Student Workbook

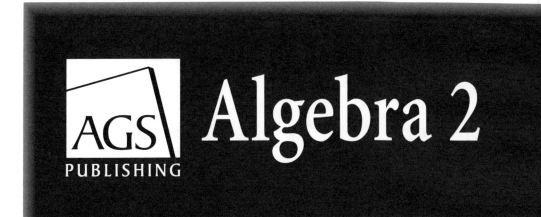

AGS Publishing
Circle Pines, MN 55014-1796
800-328-2560

© 2004 AGS Publishing
4201 Woodland Road
Circle Pines, MN 55014-1796
800-328-2560 • www.agsnet.com

AGS Publishing is a trademark and trade name of American Guidance Service, Inc.

Printed in the United States of America

ISBN 0-7854-3545-X

Product Number 93843

A 0 9 8 7 6 5 4 3 2

Table of Contents

Writing Equations

> **EXAMPLE** One-half of a number plus 3 is 13.
>
> $\frac{1}{2}x + 3 = 13$

Directions Write an equation for each statement. Let x be the number.

1. 6 times a number is 18.   _____

2. One-fifth of a number is 25.   _____

3. 8 plus some number is 22.   _____

4. Two-thirds of a number is 12.   _____

5. 4 times a number plus 4 is twice the number.   _____

6. A number plus one-fourth of the number is 150.   _____

7. 3 times a number subtracted from 45 is 30.   _____

8. 14 less than one-half of a number is 2 more than the number.   _____

Directions Circle the equation that solves the problem.

9. Sandra rode her bike 54 miles in one day. She rode 6 times the number of miles Caleb rode his bike. How many miles did Caleb ride his bike? Let b represent the number of miles Caleb rode his bike.

A $b = 54 - 6$

B $54b = 6$

C $6b = 54$

10. Jordan went to Europe for vacation. He spent $\frac{2}{3}$ of his time in Spain. If he was in Spain for 14 days, how long was he in Europe? Let v represent the number of days he was in Europe.

A $\frac{2}{3}v = 14$

B $\frac{2}{3}(14) = v$

C $v \div 14 = \frac{2}{3}$

Axioms of Equality (Rules for Equations)

Directions Draw a line to match the axiom of equality on the left with the statement on the right.

1. Reflexive Law

2. Symmetric Law

3. Transitive Law

4. Substitution Principle

A If $a = b$, then $b = a$.

B Things that are equal to the same thing are equal to each other.

C Equals may be substituted for equals. If $a = b$, then b can be substituted for a in any mathematical statement without changing its truth or falsehood.

D Anything is equal to itself.

$\boxed{\text{EXAMPLE}}$ If $3x = 15$ and $\frac{1}{2}y = 15$, then $3x = \frac{1}{2}y$.
This statement illustrates the *transitive law*.

Directions Write the axiom of equality that is illustrated.

5. $14 = 2x$ and $2x = 14$ _____

6. $23y - 6 = 23y - 6$ _____

7. $x = y$ and $4x = 17$; $4y = 17$ _____

8. If $9m = 12$ and $n = 12$, then $9m = n$ _____

9. $x = y$ and $\frac{1}{3}y = 18$; then $\frac{1}{3}x = 18$ _____

10. $x + 8 = 12$ and $12 = x + 8$ _____

11. $18 - \frac{2}{3}x = 15$ and $x = 3y$; then $18 - \frac{2}{3}(3y) = 15$ _____

Directions Complete each statement to illustrate the axiom of equality given.

12. Substitution Principle: If $a = b$ and $b + 2 = 6$, then $a +$ _____ $= 6$

13. Reflexive Law: $8y + 3 =$ _____ $+ 3$

14. Symmetric Law: If $3x - 7 = 15$, then $15 =$ _____

15. Transitive Law: If $5x + 3 = 7$ and $4x = 7$, then $5x + 3 =$ _____

Solutions by Addition or Subtraction

EXAMPLE   Write the missing step in solving the equation $x + 1 = 3$.

$x + 1$	$=$	3		$x + 1$	$=$	3
$?$	$=$	$?$		-1	$=$	-1
$x + 0$	$=$	2		$x + 0$	$=$	2

Directions   Write the missing step in solving each equation.

1. $x - 7 \quad = \quad 12$

    _____ $= $ _____

    $x + 0 \quad = \quad 19$

2. $x + 9 \quad = \quad 1$

    _____ $=$ _____

    $x + 0 \quad = \quad -8$

3. $x + 11 \quad = \quad -33$

    _____ $=$ _____

    $x + 0 \quad = \quad -44$

4. $8.5 + x \quad = \quad 12$

    _____ $=$ _____

    $0 + x \quad = \quad 3.5$

5. $x + 1\frac{1}{2} \quad = \quad 14\frac{1}{2}$

    _____ $=$ _____

    $x + 0 \quad = \quad 13$

6. $x - \frac{2}{3} \quad = \quad 5$

    _____ $=$ _____

    $x + 0 \quad = \quad 5\frac{2}{3}$

7. $x + \frac{1}{7} \quad = \quad -\frac{2}{7}$

    _____ $=$ _____

    $x + 0 \quad = \quad -\frac{3}{7}$

8. $8\frac{2}{3} + x \quad = \quad 5\frac{1}{3}$

    _____ $=$ _____

    $0 + x \quad = \quad -3\frac{1}{3}$

EXAMPLE   Solve for x: $x - 14 = 3$
                $+ 14 = +14$
                     $x = 17$

Check: Let $x = 17$; $x - 14 = 3 \rightarrow$
         $17 - 14 = 3 \rightarrow 3 = 3$
         True.

Directions   Solve each equation for x. Use the substitution principle to check your answers.

9. $x + 10 = 27$ _____

10. $x - 12 = 7$ _____

11. $x - 3\frac{1}{2} = -8$ _____

12. $19 + x = 9$ _____

13. $\frac{1}{2} + x = -2$ _____

14. $16 - x = 8$ _____

15. $x + \frac{1}{3} = 9$ _____

16. $-8.7 + x = 12$ _____

17. $x - 0.8 = -2.3$ _____

18. $5 - x = 20\frac{1}{4}$ _____

19. $x - 16.6 = -3.4$ _____

20. $-9\frac{2}{3} - x = -1\frac{1}{3}$ _____

Solutions by Multiplication or Division

EXAMPLE Write how to use the rule for multiplication or division to solve $3x = 18$.

Multiply by $\frac{1}{3}$ or divide by 3.

Directions Write how you can use the rule for multiplication or division to solve the equation.

1. $6x = 12$ multiply by _____ or divide by _____

2. $\frac{1}{3}x = 15$ multiply by _____ or divide by _____

3. $-7x = 21$ multiply by _____ or divide by _____

4. $\frac{2}{3}x = 15$ multiply by _____ or divide by _____

5. $-\frac{1}{2}x = 4$ multiply by _____ or divide by _____

EXAMPLE Solve for x: $\frac{1}{2}x = 14$ Check: Let $x = 28$; $\frac{1}{2}x = 14 \rightarrow$

$(2)(\frac{1}{2}x) = (2)(14)$ $\frac{1}{2}(28) = 14 \rightarrow 14 = 14$

$x = 28$ True.

Directions Solve for x. Use the substitution principle to check your answers.

6. $9x = 36$ _____ **11.** $\frac{1}{4}x = 2$ _____

7. $10x = 50$ _____ **12.** $-\frac{3}{2}x = 12$ _____

8. $18x = 6$ _____ **13.** $\frac{1}{10}x = 45$ _____

9. $-7x = 49$ _____ **14.** $\frac{1}{1,000}x = 8.35$ _____

10. $-8x = -4$ _____ **15.** $-\frac{1}{4}x = \frac{1}{2}$ _____

Directions Solve each problem.

16. 8 times what number equals 24? _____

17. 12 times what number equals 4? _____

18. 25 times what number equals 5? _____

19. $\frac{1}{3}$ of what number is 9? _____

20. $\frac{2}{5}$ of what number is 1? _____

Multistep Solutions

Directions One step is missing in the solution to each equation.
Using a complete sentence, write the missing step.

1. $8x - 18 = 46$

Step 1 Add 18 to both sides of the equation.

Step 2 _____

2. $-\frac{1}{4}x + 16 = -4$

Step 1 Subtract 16 from both sides of the equation.

Step 2 _____

3. $\frac{1}{5}x - 12 = 18$

Step 1 _____

Step 2 Multiply both sides of the equation by 5 (or divide by $\frac{1}{5}$).

4. $\frac{2}{3}x + 6 = 24$

Step 1 Subtract 6 from both sides of the equation.

Step 2 _____

EXAMPLE

Solve for x: $9x + 16 = 43$
$$9x + 16 = 43$$
$$9x + 16 - 16 = 43 - 16$$
$$9x = 27$$
$$(\tfrac{1}{9})(9x) = (27)(\tfrac{1}{9})$$
$$x = 3$$

Check: Let $x = 3$; $9x + 16 = 43 \rightarrow 9(3) + 16 = 43 \rightarrow$
$27 + 16 = 43 \rightarrow 43 = 43$
True.

Directions Solve each equation. Use the substitution principle to check
your answers.

5. $5x + 3 = 18$ _____

6. $30 - 5x = 0$ _____

7. $17 - 3x = 11$ _____

8. $22x + 5 = 93$ _____

9. $7 + 4x = 11$ _____

10. $3 + 6x = 21$ _____

11. $4x - 10 = 26$ _____

12. $-3x + 7 = -14$ _____

13. $\frac{1}{2}x - 12 = 16$ _____

14. $35 - \frac{2}{3}x = 13$ _____

15. $-\frac{1}{10}x + 8 = 46$ _____

16. $\frac{4}{5}x + 4 = 8$ _____

17. $-\frac{2}{7}x - 6 = -4$ _____

18. $-9x - 9 = -9$ _____

19. $-\frac{5}{6}x - 3 = 27$ _____

20. $\frac{5}{3}x - 18 = -43$ _____

Axioms of Inequality and Real Number Line

Directions On the line beside each inequality, write the letter of the
graph from the right column that matches the inequality.

1. _____ $4 - x > 0$

A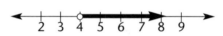

2. _____ $x - 2 < 0$

B

3. _____ $3x + 6 > 0$

C

4. _____ $18 + 6x < 0$

D

5. _____ $4x - 4 > 0$

E

6. _____ $-2 - x > 0$

F

7. _____ $100 - 20x < 0$

G

EXAMPLE Solve for x. Graph the solution.

$$8 - 2x < 0$$
$$8 - 2x - 8 < 0 - 8$$
$$-2x < -8$$
$$\left(-\tfrac{1}{2}\right)(-2x) > (-8)\left(-\tfrac{1}{2}\right)$$
$$x > 4$$

Directions Solve each inequality for x. Graph each solution on the
number line provided.

8. $x + 6 > 0$

9. $12x - 48 < 0$

10. $9x - 18 > 0$

11. $\tfrac{1}{2}x + 8 > 0$

12. $-24 - 6x > 0$

13. $25 - 100x < 0$

14. $45x + 90 < 0$

15. $-\tfrac{4}{3}x - 16 > 0$

Comparing Pairs of Numbers

Directions For each ordered pair of numbers, write whether $y < x$, $y = x$, or $y > x$.

1. $(4, -1)$ _____

2. $(-5, 6)$ _____

3. $(-4, -4)$ _____

4. $(-2, 3)$ _____

5. $(-8, -7)$ _____

6. $(19, -19)$ _____

7. $(\frac{1}{2}, -\frac{1}{4})$ _____

8. $(3\frac{1}{2}, -4)$ _____

9. $(-3, 2.5)$ _____

EXAMPLES

$(3, 5)$ lies above the equals line.

$(-2, -2)$ lies on the equals line.

$(-1, -2)$ lies below the equals line.

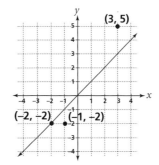

Directions Write *above*, *below*, or *on* to tell where each point lies in relation to the equals line on the coordinate plane.

10. $(-2, 3)$ _____

11. $(7, -4)$ _____

12. $(0, 4)$ _____

13. $(8, -8)$ _____

14. $(-3, -3)$ _____

15. $(0, 0)$ _____

16. $(-4, 2)$ _____

17. $(-14, -12)$ _____

18. $(7.2, -6.9)$ _____

19. $(-42, -50)$ _____

20. $(102, 102)$ _____

21. $(-\frac{1}{2}, -\frac{3}{4})$ _____

Directions Write a value for the missing coordinate in each pair to make each statement true.

22. $(-3, \_\_\_)$ lies on the equals line.

23. $(\_\_\_, -6)$ lies above the equals line.

24. $(0, \_\_\_)$ lies below the equals line.

25. $(\_\_\_, -18)$ lies below the equals line.

Intervals on the Real Number Line

Directions On the line beside each inequality, write the letter of the graphed interval from the right column that matches the inequality.

1. _____ $x < 1$ or $x > 3$

2. _____ $-3 \leq x \leq 3$

3. _____ $x > 2$ or $x < 2$

4. _____ $x \leq -3$ or $x \geq 1$

5. _____ $0 \leq x \leq 4$

6. _____ $x > 4$ or $x < 0$

7. _____ $-3 < x < 1$

EXAMPLE Write an inequality for the interval shown.

$3 \leq x \leq -4$

Directions Write an inequality for each interval.

8. 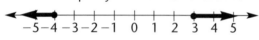 _____

9. _____

10. _____

11. _____

12. _____

13. _____

14. _____

15. 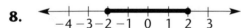 _____

Solutions of Absolute Value Equations

EXAMPLE   For $|x| = 15$, $x = 15$ or $x = -15$.

Directions Write all the values for x that make each statement true.

1. $|x| = 9$ $x =$ _____ or $x =$ _____

2. $|x| = 7$ $x =$ _____ or $x =$ _____

3. $|x| = 42$ $x =$ _____ or $x =$ _____

4. $|x| = 2\frac{1}{2}$ $x =$ _____ or $x =$ _____

5. $|x| = \frac{1}{4}$ $x =$ _____ or $x =$ _____

EXAMPLE   For $|x - 6| = 8$, $x - 6 = 8$ or $x - 6 = -8$.

Directions Write the two equations that you need to solve to find the solution of each absolute value equation.

6. $|x + 3| = 6$ _____ or _____

7. $|x - 9| = 5$ _____ or _____

8. $|x - \frac{1}{2}| = 4$ _____ or _____

9. $|x + 3\frac{1}{4}| = 7\frac{3}{4}$ _____ or _____

10. $|x + 1.3| = 8.5$ _____ or _____

EXAMPLES

$\|x\| = 8$	$\|x + 2\| = 10$	$\|4x - 1\| = 15$
$x = 8$ or $x = -8$	$x + 2 = 10$ or $x + 2 = -10$	$4x - 1 = 15$ or $4x - 1 = -15$
	$x + 2 - 2 = 10 - 2$ or	$4x - 1 + 1 = 15 + 1$ or
	$x + 2 - 2 = -10 - 2$	$4x - 1 + 1 = -15 + 1$
	$x = 8$ or $x = -12$	$4x = 16$ or $4x = -14$

$(\frac{1}{4})(4x) = (16)(\frac{1}{4})$ or $(\frac{1}{4})(4x) = (-14)(\frac{1}{4})$

$x = \frac{16}{4} = 4$ or $x = \frac{-14}{4} = -3\frac{1}{2}$

Directions Solve for x. Use the substitution principle to check your answers.

11. $|x| = 25$ _____

12. $|x + 6| = 10$ _____

13. $|x - 17| = 25$ _____

14. $|2x + 3| = 5$ _____

15. $|7x - 2| = 12$ _____

16. $|12 + 4x| = 16$ _____

17. $|3x - 10| = 17$ _____

18. $|65 + 5x| = 10$ _____

19. $|17x - 1| = 0$ _____

20. $|\frac{2}{3}x + 4| = 18$ _____

Solutions of Absolute Value Inequalities

Directions On the line beside each absolute value inequality, write the letter of the graph from the right column that matches the inequality.

1. _____ $|x + 2| \geq 5$

2. _____ $|x - 3| < 1$

3. _____ $|2x - 1| \leq 3$

4. _____ $|3x + 6| > 0$

5. _____ $|4x - 4| > 12$

6. _____ $|x - 1| \geq 1$

7. _____ $|10x - 5| < 15$

8. _____ $|4x - 2| > 6$

A $\quad$ number line from -6 to 2

B $\quad$ number line from -4 to 3

C $\quad$ number line from -10 to 6

D $\quad$ number line from -6 to 8

E $\quad$ number line from -4 to 3

F $\quad$ number line from -2 to 5

G $\quad$ number line from -3 to 5

H $\quad$ number line from -4 to 3

EXAMPLE   Solve for x. Graph.   number line from -5 to 3

$|5x + 10| \geq 10$

$$
\begin{array}{ccc}
5x + 10 \geq 10 & \text{or} & 5x + 10 \leq -10 \\
5x + 10 - 10 \geq 10 - 10 & \text{or} & 5x + 10 - 10 \leq -10 - 10 \\
5x \geq 0 & \text{or} & 5x \leq -20 \\
(\tfrac{1}{5})(5x) \geq (\tfrac{1}{5})(0) & \text{or} & (\tfrac{1}{5})(5x) \leq (\tfrac{1}{5})(-20) \\
x \geq 0 & \text{or} & x \leq -4
\end{array}
$$

Directions Solve each inequality for x. Graph each solution on the number line provided.

9. $|x| \geq 5$

10. $|3x| < 9$

11. $|12x| \leq 36$

12. $|x - 1| > 4$

13. $|x + 5| \leq 10$

14. $|4x - 8| < 12$

15. $|\tfrac{1}{2}x - 4| > 2$

Geometry Connection: Relating Lines

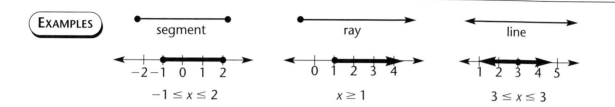

EXAMPLES

segment   ray   line

$-1 \leq x \leq 2$ $x \geq 1$ $3 \leq x \leq 3$

Directions Draw a geometric picture that fits with each algebra statement. Tell whether the picture is a line, ray, or segment.

1. $x \leq 4$ _____

2. $x \geq 3$ or $x \leq -3$ _____

3. $x \leq 0$ or $x \geq 0$ _____

4. $-3 \leq x \leq 20$ _____

5. $x \geq 57$ _____

6. $1 \leq x \leq 100$ _____

7. $x \leq -0.783$ or $x \geq 0.783$ _____

8. $x \geq 100$ or $x \leq 100$ _____

9. $x \leq -5.6$ _____

10. $-99 \leq x \leq 10$ _____

Directions Write whether the graph of the solution set of each equation or inequality below is a point, two points, a line, a ray, two rays, or a segment.

11. $x \geq 4$ _____

12. $x \leq -45$ _____

13. $|x| \leq 1$ _____

14. $x \geq -\frac{4}{3}$ _____

15. $|x| \geq 0$ _____

16. $|x| \leq 8$ _____

17. $x + 2 = 7$ _____

18. $|x + 2| = 7$ _____

19. $x + 2 \leq 5$ _____

20. $|x| = 12$ _____

21. $|x| \geq 5$ _____

22. $|x + 3| = 7$ _____

23. $|x + 3| \geq 7$ _____

24. $3x - 5 = 13$ _____

25. $3x - 5 \geq 13$ _____

26. $|3x - 5| \geq 13$ _____

27. $|3x - 5| \leq 13$ _____

28. $x + 3 = 3$ _____

29. $6 - 2x = 10$ _____

30. $6 - 2x \geq 10$ _____

Functions as Ordered Pairs

(EXAMPLE) Is this set of ordered pairs a function?
(5, 4), (7, 2), (9, 0), (11, −2)
The set of ordered pairs is a function because no *x*-coordinates have been repeated.

Directions Tell whether the sets of ordered pairs are functions or not.
Write *yes* or *no* and explain your answer.

1. $(1, 0), (4, 2), (7, 4), (10, 6)$

_____

2. $(5, -2), (5, -1), (5, 0), (5, 1)$

_____

3. $(-3, 3), (-2, 2), (-1, 1), (0, 0)$

_____

4. $(9, -2), (8, 1), (7, 4), (6, 7)$

_____

5. $(0, 0), (-1, 2), (1, 0), (1, 2)$

_____

Directions If a vertical line passes through two or more points of a graph,
the graph does not represent a function. Use this vertical line
test to determine if the graph is a function or not.
Write *yes* or *no*.

6.

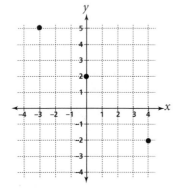

7.

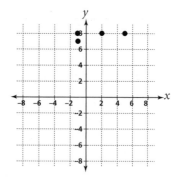

(EXAMPLE) Write the domain and range of this function.
(7, −2), (1, 4), (3, 6), (−4, −1)
The domain is 7, 1, 3, −4. The range is −2, 4, 6, −1.

Directions Write the domain and range for each function below.

8. $(1, -2), (0, 2), (-1, 6), (-2, 10)$ _____

9. $(5, 0), (3, -2), (1, -4), (-1, -6)$ _____

10. $(0, 4), (2, -1), (4, -6), (-2, 8)$ _____

Functions as a Rule

EXAMPLE   Calculate $f(x)$ for the given domain values.
$f(x) = 3x$; $x = 1, 3, 8, 10, 100$
$f(x) = 3, 9, 24, 30, 300$ for the given domain values.

Directions Calculate $f(x)$ for the given domain values.

1. $f(x) = 5x$; $x = 4, 6, 8, 10, 20$

2. $f(x) = -3x$; $x = 0, -1, -2, -3, -4$

3. $f(x) = \frac{1}{6}x$; $x = 6, 12, -12, -42, 60$

4. $f(x) = 5x + 2$; $x = 0, 1, 2, 3, 4$

5. $f(x) = 7x - 11$; $x = 3, 6, 9, 12, 15$

6. $f(x) = \frac{1}{2}x - 5$; $x = 0, 4, 10, 50, -100$

7. $f(x) = 4x + 8$; $x = 1, 11, 21, 31, 101$

8. $f(x) = -2x - 14$; $x = -1, -5, -10, -15, 12$

9. $f(x) = \frac{1}{3}x + 22$; $x = 9, 6, 3, 0, -3$

10. $f(x) = \frac{7}{8}x - 12$; $x = 16, 24, 48, -8, -64$

EXAMPLE   Choose any number; then multiply it by 7.

$f(x) = 7x$ is a rule in function notation for the example above.
The reason that it is a function is that each x has one and only one $7x$.

Directions Write a rule using function notation, $f(x) = $ _____.
Then give a reason why it is a function.

11. Choose any number; then divide it by 6.   _____

12. Choose any number; then multiply it by 4.   _____

13. Choose any number; multiply it by 3, then add 15.   _____

14. Choose any number; then subtract 9.   _____

15. Choose any number; then divide it by -2.   _____

16. Choose any number; then multiply it by -5.   _____

17. Choose any number; multiply it by -8, then subtract 7. _____

18. Choose any number; divide it by 3, then add 13.   _____

19. Choose any number; multiply it by 4, then subtract 52. _____

Directions Solve the problem.

20. Each month Daisy shoots eight rolls of film. Write a rule that shows
how many rolls of film she shoots for a given number of months.
Write the rule in function notation.

Zeros of a Function

EXAMPLE $f(x) = 3x - 6$ Find the zeros of $f(x)$.

Let $f(x) = 0$ and solve for x.
$$0 = 3x - 6$$
$$6 = 3x$$
$$2 = x$$

Check: $f(2) = 3(2) - 6$
$$f(2) = 6 - 6$$
$$f(2) = 0$$

Directions   Find the zeros of $f(x)$.

1. $f(x) = -2x + 12$ **16.** $f(x) = \frac{2}{7}x - 4$

2. $f(x) = \frac{2}{5}x - 10$ **17.** $f(x) = x^3 - 125$

3. $f(x) = 4x - 4$ **18.** $f(x) = \frac{3}{4}x + 12$

4. $f(x) = \frac{1}{3}x - 9$ **19.** $f(x) = 10x + 25$

5. $f(x) = x + 8$ **20.** $f(x) = x^3 - 27$

6. $f(x) = x^2 - 64$ **21.** $f(x) = 2x + 10$

7. $f(x) = \frac{1}{4}x + 3$ **22.** $f(x) = \frac{1}{10}x + 100$

8. $f(x) = 5x - 10$ **23.** $f(x) = 7x + 91$

9. $f(x) = -x - 8$ **24.** $f(x) = 6x + 15$

10. $f(x) = 6x + 42$ **25.** $f(x) = \frac{10}{21}x - 1$

11. $f(x) = 9x - 9$ **26.** $f(x) = 30x - 450$

12. $f(x) = 7x - 3$ **27.** $f(x) = x^4 - 81$

13. $f(x) = \frac{3}{8}x - 1$ **28.** $f(x) = \frac{1}{6}x + 2$

14. $f(x) = x^2 - 81$ **29.** $f(x) = 15x + 75$

15. $f(x) = 8x + 4$ **30.** $f(x) = x^5 - 32$

Graphs of Linear Functions

EXAMPLE Graph $f(x) = 3x + 5$.

Step 1 Let $x = 0$.
$f(0) = 3(0) + 5 = 5 \rightarrow (0, 5)$ is point A.
$y = 5$ is the y-intercept.

Step 2 Let $x = -1$.
$f(-1) = 3(-1) + 5 = 2 \rightarrow (-1, 2)$ is point B.

Step 3 Graph the two points; then draw the
line $y = f(x) = 3x + 5$.

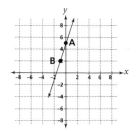

Directions Graph each linear function and label the y-intercept.
(Use graph paper. Label the x- and y-axes first.)

1. $f(x) = 2x$

2. $f(x) = 3x + 2$

3. $f(x) = -4x$

4. $f(x) = 2x - 4$

5. $f(x) = 5x + 1$

6. $f(x) = \frac{1}{4}x$

7. $f(x) = -3x - 8$

8. $f(x) = 2x + 7$

9. $f(x) = \frac{3}{8}x + 2$

10. $f(x) = 5x - 2$

11. $f(x) = \frac{2}{7}x$

12. $f(x) = 4x - 5$

13. $f(x) = -\frac{1}{5}x + 3$

14. $f(x) = x + 10$

15. $f(x) = \frac{1}{4}x - 6$

16. $f(x) = 6x + 6$

17. $f(x) = \frac{7}{10}x$

18. $f(x) = 10x - 8$

19. $f(x) = \frac{1}{5}x + 2$

20. $f(x) = 8x + 8$

The Slope of a Line, Parallel Lines

EXAMPLE   Calculate the slope of $f(x) = 3x + 4$.

Step 1 Find two points.

$f(1) = 3(1) + 4 = 7 \rightarrow (1, 7)$ is point 1.
$f(0) = 4(0) + 4 = 4 \rightarrow (0, 4)$ is point 2.

Step 2 Calculate $m = \frac{(y_1 - y_2)}{(x_1 - x_2)}$.

$m = \frac{(7 - 4)}{(1 - 0)} = \frac{3}{1} = 3$

$m = 3$

Directions Calculate the slope of each line. Remember, $m = \frac{(y_1 - y_2)}{(x_1 - x_2)}$.

1. $f(x) = x + 5$ _____

2. $f(x) = 4x - 2$ _____

3. $f(x) = -3x$ _____

4. $f(x) = 5x$ _____

5. $f(x) = -2x - 7$ _____

6. $f(x) = \frac{1}{2}x$ _____

7. $f(x) = \frac{3}{7}x + 5$ _____

8. $f(x) = -7x - 2$ _____

9. $f(x) = -\frac{2}{9}x + 1$ _____

10. $f(x) = x - 6$ _____

11. $f(x) = \frac{2}{5}x + 1$ _____

12. $f(x) = 2\frac{1}{2}x + 6$ _____

13. $f(x) = -4x - 9$ _____

14. $f(x) = -\frac{1}{15}x + 3$ _____

15. $f(x) = 10x - 1$ _____

16. $f(x) = -15x - 25$ _____

17. $f(x) = \frac{2}{15}x + 8$ _____

18. $f(x) = -4x - 11$ _____

19. $f(x) = -\frac{8}{11}x + 5$ _____

20. $f(x) = 18x + 1$ _____

EXAMPLE   Given $f(x) = 5x$ and $g(x) = 5x - 4$, show that the lines are parallel by showing that their slopes are equal.

$f(1) = 5(1) = 5 \rightarrow (1, 5)$ is point 1.
$f(0) = 5(0) = 0 \rightarrow (0, 0)$ is point 2.
$m = \frac{(5 - 0)}{(1 - 0)} = \frac{5}{1}$
$m = 5$

$g(1) = 5(1) - 4 = 1 \rightarrow (1, 1)$ is point 1.
$g(0) = 5(0) - 4 = -4 \rightarrow (0, -4)$ is point 2.
$m = \frac{(1 + 4)}{(1 - 0)} = \frac{5}{1}$
$m = 5$

Directions Show that the lines are parallel by showing that their slopes are equal.

21. $f(x) = 2x + 5$ and $g(x) = 2x$ _____

22. $f(x) = -6x$ and $g(x) = -6x + 7$ _____

23. $f(x) = \frac{1}{3}x - 4$ and $g(x) = \frac{1}{3}x + 4$ _____

24. $f(x) = -x + 100$ and $g(x) = -x - 8$ _____

Directions Solve the problem.

25. A hill has a height of 450 feet. The horizontal distance covered between the bottom of the hill and the top is 1,800 feet. Find the slope of the hill.

The Formula $f(x) = y = mx + b$

EXAMPLE

$5x + y = 2$
Change to $y = mx + b$. Give m and b.
Solution: Subtract $5x$ from both sides. $\quad y = -5x + 2$

$$m = -5, \ y\text{-intercept} = 2$$

Directions Change the given equation to the form $y = mx + b$.
Give the value of m and b.

1. $2x + 4y = 8$ _____

2. $-2x + y = 1$ _____

3. $-4x + 4y = 4$ _____

4. $-x + 3y = 9$ _____

5. $3x + y = -7$ _____

6. $-2x + 2y = 2$ _____

7. $x - 4y = 2$ _____

8. $-3x + 6y = 12$ _____

9. $4x + 8 = y$ _____

10. $-6x + 10 = y$ _____

11. $-6x - 3y = 9$ _____

12. $-\frac{1}{3}x + 6y = 2$ _____

13. $\frac{2}{5}x + \frac{1}{5}y = 5$ _____

14. $-x + \frac{1}{3}y = 4$ _____

15. $-3x + \frac{1}{5}y = -4$ _____

16. $2x + \frac{1}{5}y = 0$ _____

17. $x - \frac{1}{10}y = 1$ _____

18. $\frac{1}{5}x + 2y = 8$ _____

19. $-10x + 8 = 5y - 2$ _____

20. $\frac{1}{3}x + 9 = \frac{1}{3}y + 6$ _____

21. $-x + \frac{3}{4}y = -2$ _____

22. $-6x + 9y = 3$ _____

23. $x + \frac{1}{8}y = -4$ _____

24. $-3x - y = 6$ _____

25. $\frac{1}{2}x + 2y = 8 - 2y$ _____

26. $x + \frac{1}{6}y = 6$ _____

27. $-\frac{1}{10}x + y = 10$ _____

28. $-12x - 4y = 2y + 3$ _____

29. $-x + y = 0$ _____

30. $-x + y = 2$ _____

Reading Line Graphs: Slopes of Lines

EXAMPLE   The slope of this line is positive because it ascends to the right.
The *y*-intercept is 8 because the line crosses the *y*-axis at (0, 8).
The zero or root is −2 because the line crosses the *x*-axis at (−2, 0).

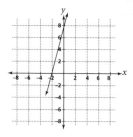

Directions Give the slope (positive, zero, or negative), the *y*-intercept,
and the zero or root for each graph.

1. _____

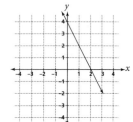

4. _____

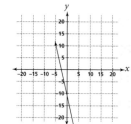

7. _____

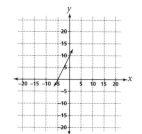

10. _____

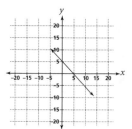

2. _____

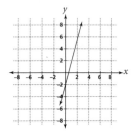

5. _____

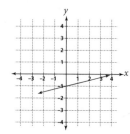

8. _____

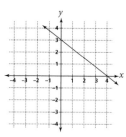

3. _____

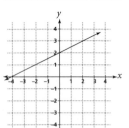

6. _____

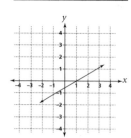

9. _____

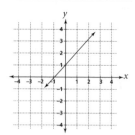

Writing Equations of Lines

EXAMPLE Write the equation of the line with $m = 2$ and y-intercept $= 7$.
$y = 2x + 7$

Directions Given m and b, write the equation of the line.

1. $m = -3; b = 4$ _____

2. $m = 1; b = 3$ _____

3. $m = 5; b = -6$ _____

4. $m = 8; b = -\frac{1}{2}$ _____

5. $m = 2; b = -2$ _____

6. $m = \frac{1}{5}; b = -5$ _____

7. $m = 4; b = 4$ _____

8. $m = -1; b = 0$ _____

9. $m = 0; b = 4$ _____

10. $m = \frac{3}{7}; b = -1$ _____

11. $m = 5; b = -\frac{5}{6}$ _____

12. $m = -\frac{1}{3}; b = 4$ _____

13. $m = -2; b = 0$ _____

14. $m = 0; b = -5$ _____

15. $m = \frac{4}{5}; b = 1\frac{1}{2}$ _____

16. $m = 0; b = 1$ _____

17. $m = 5\frac{1}{4}; b = -4$ _____

18. $m = \frac{1}{10}; b = 0$ _____

19. $m = 11; b = 11$ _____

20. $m = -4; b = 14$ _____

EXAMPLE Write the equation of a line passing through $(0, 4)$ and $(1, 1)$.

Step 1 Calculate m. Let $(x_1, y_1) = (0, 4)$ and
$(x_2, y_2) = (1, 1)$.
$m = \frac{(y_1 - y_2)}{(x_1 - x_2)} = \frac{(4 - 1)}{(0 - 1)} = \frac{3}{-1} = -3$
$m = -3$ so $y = -3x + b$

Step 2 Substitute one point in $y = -3x + b$ and solve for b.
$(0, 4) \to x = 0, y = 4$ $4 = -3(0) + b$
$4 = 0 + b$
$4 = b$

Step 3 Write the equation: $y = -3x + 4$.

Directions Write the equation of the line passing through the two points.

21. $(1, 1)$ and $(2, 6)$ _____

22. $(1, 4)$ and $(0, 5)$ _____

23. $(0, 3)$ and $(-1, 4)$ _____

24. $(2, 4)$ and $(1, 5)$ _____

25. $(3, 6)$ and $(1, 7)$ _____

26. $(5, 0)$ and $(4, -1)$ _____

27. $(-4, 1)$ and $(0, 2)$ _____

28. $(-10, 2)$ and $(-11, 3)$ _____

29. $(6, 2)$ and $(2, 6)$ _____

30. $(1, 1)$ and $(7, 6)$ _____

Graphs of $y < mx + b$, $y > mx + b$

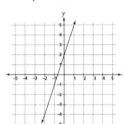 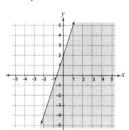 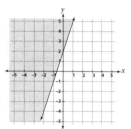

EXAMPLE $y = 3x + 2$ $y \leq 3x + 2$ $y \geq 3x + 2.$

Directions Write the inequality for the shaded region.

1. _____

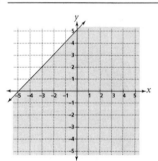

3. _____

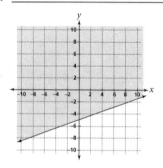

5. _____

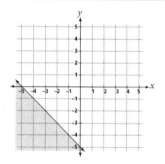

2. _____

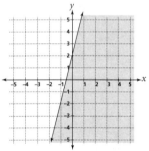

4. _____

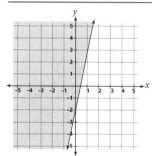

6. _____

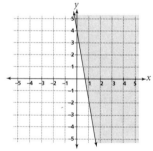

Directions Sketch each of the following inequalities in the coordinate plane.

7. $x \leq 4$ **8.** $y < 3$ **9.** $y < -4$ **10.** $y \leq 4x$

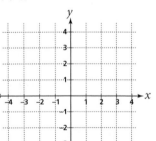 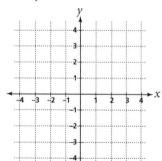 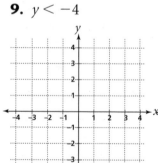 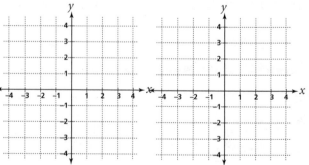

Name   Date   Period

Geometry Connection: Lines

  In algebra's coordinate plane, the
x- and y-axes are perpendicular.

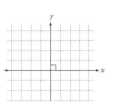

Lines that have the same slope such as
$y = x + 1$ and $y = x - 1$ are parallel.

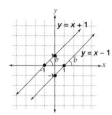

Directions Write a reason from geometry why each statement is true.

1. The line $x = 7$ is parallel to the y-axis. Why?

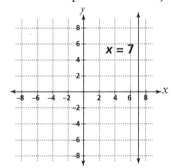

2. The line $y = -3$ is parallel to the x-axis. Why?

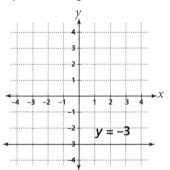

3. The vertical lines are parallel to the y-axis. Why?

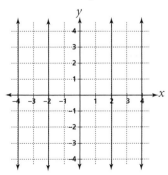

4. The horizontal lines are parallel to the x-axis. Why?

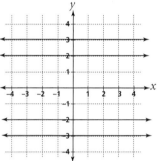

5. $y = 3x + 5$ and $y = 3x - 2$ are parallel. Why?

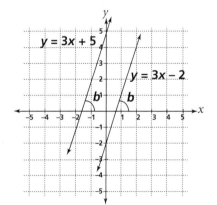

The Distributive Law—Multiplication

EXAMPLE $6(x - y) = 6x - 6y$

Directions Multiply, using the distributive law.

1. $3(8 + 2)$ _____

2. $6(x + y)$ _____

3. $a(b + c)$ _____

4. $x(a + b - c)$ _____

5. $x(3x + 9)$ _____

6. $y(x + y^3)$ _____

7. $x(a - b - c)$ _____

8. $x^2(x^3 + y^3)$ _____

9. $x^4(x + z - y)$ _____

10. $x^3(5x^3 + x^2)$ _____

EXAMPLE $(2 + 7)(y - x) = 2y - 2x + 7y - 7x$
             $= 9y - 9x$

Directions Multiply, using the distributive law twice. Simplify by adding like terms.

11. $(6 + 4)(a - b)$ _____

12. $(a - 2)(a + 4)$ _____

13. $(x + y)(a - b)$ _____

14. $(x + 3)(x + 5)$ _____

15. $(y + 4)(y - 4)$ _____

16. $(2a + 4)(a + 5)$ _____

17. $(x - y)(y - x)$ _____

18. $(a + 2b)(4a + b)$ _____

19. $(a + b)(a - b)$ _____

20. $(x - y)(3x + 3y)$ _____

EXAMPLE $(x + 3)(x - y + 8) =$
             $x^2 - xy + 8x + 3x - 3y + 24 =$
             $x^2 - xy + 11x - 3y + 24$

Directions Multiply.

21. $(x - 5)(x - y + 4)$ _____

22. $(x + y)(6x + y - z)$ _____

23. $(x + y)(3x^2 + 4y + 7)$ _____

24. $(x - 4)(4x + y + z)$ _____

25. $(a - b)(3a + 6b + ab)$ _____

26. $(a + b)(a^3 - b^2 + 1)$ _____

27. $(a - b)(a + 2b - 4ab)$ _____

28. $(x + 3)(3x - y + 8)$ _____

29. $(x + 4y)(x - y + xy)$ _____

30. $(x + y)(x + y - 10)$ _____

The Distributive Law—Factoring

EXAMPLES
$rb + rc = r(b + c)$

$3yx^2 + 6yx - 9y^2 = 3y(x^2 + 2x - 3y)$

Directions Factor the expressions by finding the common factor(s) first.

1. $kl + kj$

2. $9x + 6y$

3. $x^2 - xy - x$

4. $xb - xc + xd$

5. $2x^2 - 6xy + 4x$

6. $ab - ac + a^3$

7. $axy - xy^2$

8. $5xy + 10xya$

9. $4x^2y + 12xy + 10y^2$

10. $g^2 + g^3$

EXAMPLE
Factor $x^2 + 6x + 9$.

Step 1 $x^2 + 6x + 9 = (x + \underline{\ \ })(x + \underline{\ \ })$

Step 2 The factors of 9 are 3 and 3; 1 and 9; -3 and -3; and -1 and -9.
So the possible factors for $x^2 + 6x + 9$ include
$(x + 3)(x + 3)$; $(x + 1)(x + 9)$; $(x - 3)(x - 3)$; and $(x - 1)(x - 9)$.

Step 3 Substitute each set of factors in the product and check.
$$x^2 + 6x + 9 = (x - 1)(x - 9)$$
$$= x(x - 9) - 1(x - 9)$$
$$= x^2 - 9x - x + 9$$
$$= x^2 - 10x + 9 \ \text{Incorrect.}$$

$$x^2 + 6x + 9 = (x + 3)(x + 3)$$
$$= x(x + 3) + 3(x + 3)$$
$$= x^2 + 3x + 3x + 9$$
$$= x^2 + 6x + 9 \ \text{Correct.}$$

Directions Factor, using the model $(x + \underline{\ \ })(x + \underline{\ \ })$.
Check by multiplying.

11. $x^2 + 7x + 6$

12. $x^2 + x - 6$

13. $x^2 + 8x + 15$

14. $x^2 - 2x - 15$

15. $x^2 + 2x - 8$

16. $x^2 + 3x - 18$

17. $x^2 - 25$

18. $x^2 + 6x + 5$

19. $x^2 + 6x - 7$

20. $x^2 - 10x + 25$

Solutions to $ax^2 + bx = 0$

EXAMPLE Solve for x and check: $2x^2 + 8x = 0$.

Step 1 Factor: $2x^2 + 8x = 0 \rightarrow 2x(x + 4) = 0$

Step 2 Set each factor equal to 0 and solve for x:
$2x = 0$ or $x + 4 = 0$
$x = 0$ or $x = -4$

Check:
$x = 0,\ 2x^2 + 8x = 0 \rightarrow 2(0)^2 + 8(0) = 0 + 0 = 0$
$x = -4,\ 2x^2 + 8x = 0 \rightarrow 2(-4)^2 + 8(-4) = 32 - 32 = 0$

Directions Solve for x and check.

1. $x^2 + 12x = 0$ _____

2. $x^2 - 3x = 0$ _____

3. $x^2 - 10x = 0$ _____

4. $x^2 + 25x = 0$ _____

5. $x^2 - 13x = 0$ _____

6. $x^2 - 7x = 0$ _____

7. $x^2 - 19x = 0$ _____

8. $x^2 + 23x = 0$ _____

9. $x^2 + 36x = 0$ _____

10. $x^2 - 45x = 0$ _____

11. $2x^2 - 8x = 0$ _____

12. $3x^2 - 15x = 0$ _____

13. $4x^2 + 4x = 0$ _____

14. $10x^2 - 25x = 0$ _____

15. $8x^2 + 16x = 0$ _____

16. $6x^2 - 21x = 0$ _____

17. $2x^2 + 40x = 0$ _____

18. $3x^2 + 30x = 0$ _____

19. $4x^2 - 36x = 0$ _____

20. $5x^2 - 45x = 0$ _____

21. $2x^2 + 48x = 0$ _____

22. $3x^2 + 48x = 0$ _____

23. $4x^2 - 52x = 0$ _____

24. $5x^2 + 75x = 0$ _____

25. $6x^2 - 90x = 0$ _____

26. $12x^2 - 6x = 0$ _____

27. $20x^2 + 4x = 0$ _____

28. $15x^2 - 3x = 0$ _____

29. $24x^2 + 6x = 0$ _____

30. $35x^2 + 7x = 0$ _____

Solutions to $x^2 + bx + c = 0$ by Factoring

EXAMPLE

Solve for x by factoring $x^2 + 7x + 10 = 0$. Then check.

Step 1 Factor: $x^2 + 7x + 10 = 0$

$(x + \_\_)(x + \_\_) = 0$ Think: Factors of 10 are 2, 5, 1, 10.

$(x + 2)(x + 5) = 0$

Step 2 Set each factor equal to 0: $x + 2 = 0$ or $x + 5 = 0$

Solve for x: $x = -2$ or $x = -5$

Check:

$x = -2$, $x^2 + 7x + 10 = 0 \rightarrow (-2)^2 + 7(-2) + 10 = 4 - 14 + 10 = 0$

$x = -5$, $x^2 + 7x + 10 = 0 \rightarrow (-5)^2 + 7(-5) + 10 = 25 - 35 + 10 = 0$

Directions Solve for x by factoring. Check your answers.

1. $x^2 + 2x - 8 = 0$ _____

2. $x^2 + 2x - 15 = 0$ _____

3. $x^2 - 6x + 9 = 0$ _____

4. $x^2 + 3x - 18 = 0$ _____

5. $x^2 + 4x - 21 = 0$ _____

6. $x^2 - 10x + 25 = 0$ _____

7. $x^2 + 9x + 14 = 0$ _____

8. $x^2 + 3x - 10 = 0$ _____

9. $x^2 + 5x - 6 = 0$ _____

10. $x^2 + 6x - 27 = 0$ _____

11. $x^2 + 11x - 26 = 0$ _____

12. $x^2 + 12x + 35 = 0$ _____

13. $x^2 + 14x + 45 = 0$ _____

14. $x^2 + 2x - 80 = 0$ _____

15. $x^2 + 20x + 100 = 0$ _____

16. $x^2 - 6x - 55 = 0$ _____

17. $x^2 - 8x - 33 = 0$ _____

18. $x^2 + 8x - 65 = 0$ _____

19. $x^2 - 13x + 36 = 0$ _____

20. $x^2 - 14x + 40 = 0$ _____

21. $x^2 + 30x + 29 = 0$ _____

22. $x^2 - 9x - 52 = 0$ _____

23. $x^2 + 16x + 64 = 0$ _____

24. $x^2 + 19x + 84 = 0$ _____

25. $x^2 - 20x - 69 = 0$ _____

26. $x^2 + 3x - 70 = 0$ _____

27. $x^2 + 17x + 30 = 0$ _____

28. $x^2 - x - 56 = 0$ _____

29. $x^2 - x - 72 = 0$ _____

30. $x^2 - 3x - 108 = 0$ _____

Solutions to $ax^2 + bx + c = 0$ by Factoring

EXAMPLE Solve for x by factoring $2x^2 + 6x + 4 = 0$. Then check.

Step 1 Factor: $2x^2 + 6x + 4 = 0$
$(\_x + \_)(\_x + \_) = 0$ Factors of 2: 2 and 1
Factors of 4: 2, 2, 1, and 4
Some trial factors:

$(2x + 1)(x + 4) = 0$ $(2x + 2)(x + 2)$
$= 2x(x + 4) + 1(x + 4)$ $= 2x(x + 2) + 2(x + 2)$
$= 2x^2 + 8x + x + 4$ $= 2x^2 + 4x + 2x + 4$
$= 2x^2 + 9x + 4$ $= 2x^2 + 6x + 4$
No   Yes
The factors of $2x^2 + 6x + 4 = 0$ are $(2x + 2)$ and $(x + 2)$.

Step 2 Set each factor equal to 0: $2x + 2 = 0$ or $x + 2 = 0$
Solve for x: $2x = -2$ or $x = -2$
$x = -1$ or $x = -2$

Check: Let $x = -1$ and   Let $x = -2$ and
$2x^2 + 6x + 4 = 0$ $2x^2 + 6x + 4 = 0$
$2(-1)^2 + 6(-1) + 4 = 0$ $2(-2)^2 + 6(-2) + 4 = 0$
$2(1) - 6 + 4 = 0$ $2(4) - 12 + 4 = 0$
$2 - 6 + 4 = 0$ $8 - 12 + 4 = 0$
$0 = 0$ $0 = 0$

Directions Solve each equation by factoring. Check your answers.

1. $2x^2 + 7x + 6 = 0$
2. $3x^2 + 8x + 4 = 0$
3. $4x^2 + 17x + 4 = 0$
4. $6x^2 + 12x + 6 = 0$
5. $2x^2 + 2x - 4 = 0$
6. $6x^2 + 11x - 10 = 0$
7. $2x^2 + 2x - 12 = 0$
8. $8x^2 + 10x + 3 = 0$
9. $4x^2 - 25 = 0$
10. $4x^2 + 9x + 5 = 0$
11. $2x^2 - 3x - 2 = 0$
12. $12x^2 + 9x - 3 = 0$
13. $9x^2 - 16 = 0$
14. $4x^2 - 4x - 8 = 0$
15. $6x^2 - 32x + 10 = 0$
16. $8x^2 - 18x + 7 = 0$
17. $6x^2 + 3x - 9 = 0$
18. $6x^2 + x - 1 = 0$
19. $4x^2 + 14x - 8 = 0$
20. $6x^2 - 13x - 15 = 0$
21. $6x^2 + 22x + 20 = 0$
22. $6x^2 + 37x + 6 = 0$
23. $5x^2 + 26x + 5 = 0$
24. $4x^2 + 13x + 3 = 0$
25. $2x^2 + 3x - 9 = 0$
26. $6x^2 - 5x - 21 = 0$
27. $6x^2 - 3x - 18 = 0$
28. $10x^2 - 99x - 10 = 0$
29. $12x^2 + 25x + 2 = 0$
30. $15x^2 + 14x + 3 = 0$

Trinomials—Completing the Square

EXAMPLE

monomial	one term	a, b, cd, e^2, and so on
binomial	two terms	$x + 7$, $xy + 2$, $(x^2 + 6)$
trinomial	three terms	$x^2 + 4x + 3$, $2x^2 + 5x + 2$
polynomial	many terms	$3x^2 + 7x + 6y - 2z^2 + 5$

Directions Identify each expression. Write *monomial*, *binominal*, *trinomial*, or *polynomial*.

1. $10x^2$ _____

2. $x^2 - 4$ _____

3. $5x + 4y$ _____

4. $5x^2 + 6x - 3y + 8$ _____

5. $6x^2 + 2x - 9$ _____

6. $2x^2 - 5x + 2$ _____

7. 52 _____

8. $5x^2 + 3x$ _____

9. $6x^2 + 13x + 2$ _____

10. $a + b + c + d$ _____

EXAMPLE

Complete the square, given $x^2 + 10x +$ ___. Check.

Solution: Find $\frac{1}{2}$ of $10 = 5$. Square 5 and add to given expression.

$x^2 + 10x + 25$, perfect square trinomial

$x^2 + 10x + 25$

$(x \quad + \quad 5)^2$

Check: $(x + 5)^2 = (x + 5)(x + 5) = x(x + 5) + 5(x + 5) = x^2 + 5x + 5x + 25 = x^2 + 10x + 25$

Directions Complete the square. Check by factoring and multiplying.

11. $x^2 + 40x$ _____

12. $x^2 + 30x$ _____

13. $x^2 - 12x$ _____

14. $x^2 - 18x$ _____

15. $x^2 + 26x$ _____

16. $x^2 - 26x$ _____

17. $x^2 - 40x$ _____

18. $x^2 + 22x$ _____

19. $x^2 - 30x$ _____

20. $x^2 - 2x$ _____

Solutions by Completing the Square

EXAMPLE   Solve $x^2 + 12x - 13 = 0$ by completing the square.

Solution:

$$x^2 + 12x - 13 = 0$$
$$x^2 + 12x = 13 \qquad \text{Change to } x + bx = \text{constant.}$$
$$x^2 + 12x + 36 = 13 + 36 \qquad \text{Complete the square. Add } [\tfrac{1}{2}(b)]^2 \text{ to both sides.}$$
$$(x + 6)^2 = 49 \qquad \text{Factor.}$$
$$\sqrt{(x + 6)^2} = \pm\sqrt{49} \qquad \text{Take the square root of each side.}$$
$$x + 6 = \pm 7$$
$$x + 6 = 7 \text{ or } x + 6 = -7$$
$$x = 1 \text{ or } x = -13$$

Check:

Let $x = 1$
$x^2 + 12x - 13 = 0 \rightarrow 1 + 12 - 13 = 0 \rightarrow 13 - 13 = 0 \rightarrow 0 = 0$
Let $x = -13$
$x^2 + 12x - 13 = 0 \rightarrow 169 - 156 - 13 = 0 \rightarrow 169 - 169 = 0 \rightarrow 0 = 0$

Directions Solve by completing the square. Check your answers.

1. $x^2 + 12x + 11 = 0$ _____

2. $x^2 + 10x + 9 = 0$ _____

3. $x^2 + 8x - 20 = 0$ _____

4. $x^2 + 16x + 28 = 0$ _____

5. $x^2 + 18x - 19 = 0$ _____

6. $x^2 + 4x - 12 = 0$ _____

EXAMPLE   Solve $x^2 + 4x - 2 = 0$ by completing the square.

Solution:

$$x^2 + 4x - 2 = 0$$
$$x^2 + 4x = 2 \qquad \text{Change to } x + bx = \text{constant.}$$
$$x^2 + 4x + 4 = 2 + 4 \qquad \text{Complete the square. Add } [\tfrac{1}{2}(b)]^2 \text{ to both sides.}$$
$$(x + 2)^2 = 6 \qquad \text{Factor.}$$
$$\sqrt{(x + 2)^2} = \pm\sqrt{6} \qquad \text{Take the square root of each side.}$$
$$x + 2 = \pm\sqrt{6}$$
$$x + 2 = +\sqrt{6} \text{ or } x + 2 = -\sqrt{6}$$
$$x = -2 + \sqrt{6} \text{ or } x = -2 - \sqrt{6}$$

Directions Solve by completing the square. Check your answers. You may leave expressions for square roots in your answers.

7. $x^2 + 14x - 9 = 0$ _____

8. $x^2 + 16x - 10 = 0$ _____

9. $x^2 - 18x + 11 = 0$ _____

10. $x^2 - 20x - 12 = 0$ _____

The Quadratic Formula

EXAMPLE   You can rewrite any quadratic equation that is not in standard form
so that it is in standard form, $ax^2 + bx + c = 0$.

$10x^2 - 15 = -19x$; standard form is $10x^2 + 19x - 15 = 0$.

Directions Rewrite in standard form.

1. $x^2 = -6x + 4$ _____

2. $3x + 6 = 10x^2$ _____

3. $2x^2 + 2x = 27$ _____

4. $25x + 9 = 11x^2$ _____

5. $15x^2 + 4x = -18$ _____

6. $2x^2 + 26x = 54$ _____

7. $4x^2 = 70x - 15$ _____

8. $2x^2 = 4 + 5x$ _____

9. $5 = 3x^2 - 16x$ _____

10. $3x^2 = x - 36$ _____

EXAMPLE   Solve $2x^2 + 9x + 4 = 0$ by using the quadratic formula $x = \frac{-b \pm \sqrt{b^2 - 4ac}}{2a}$.

$a = 2$, $b = 9$, $c = 4$

Substitute in the formula: $x = \frac{-9 \pm \sqrt{9^2 - 4(2)(4)}}{2(2)}$

$x = \frac{-9 \pm \sqrt{81 - 32}}{4}$

$x = \frac{-9 \pm \sqrt{49}}{4}$

$x = \frac{-9 \pm 7}{4}$

The roots of the equation are $x = \frac{-9 + 7}{4} = \frac{-2}{4} = -\frac{1}{2}$

or $x = \frac{-9 - 7}{4} = \frac{-16}{4} = -4$

Check:

Let $x = -\frac{1}{2}$; $2x^2 + 9x + 4 = 0 \rightarrow 2(-\frac{1}{2})^2 + 9(-\frac{1}{2}) + 4 = 0 \rightarrow \frac{2}{4} - \frac{9}{2} + 4 = 0$

$\rightarrow \frac{1}{2} - \frac{9}{2} + \frac{8}{2} = 0 \rightarrow 0 = 0$

Let $x = -4$; $2x^2 + 9x + 4 = 0 \rightarrow 2(-4)^2 + 9(-4) + 4 = 0 \rightarrow$

$32 - 36 + 4 = 0 \rightarrow 36 - 36 = 0 \rightarrow 0 = 0$

Directions Solve, using the quadratic formula.

11. $6x^2 + 19x + 3 = 0$ _____

12. $x^2 - 5x + 4 = 0$ _____

13. $7x^2 + 11x - 6 = 0$ _____

14. $8x^2 - 14x + 6 = 0$ _____

15. $2x^2 - 2x - 4 = 0$ _____

Complex Roots

EXAMPLE Are the roots of $2x^2 - 3x + 7 = 0$ real or complex?
$a = 2, b = -3, c = 7$
Radicand $= b^2 - 4ac$
$= (-3)^2 - 4(2)(7)$
$= 9 - 56 = -47$
Radicand < 0, so roots are complex.

Directions Evaluate the radicand $b^2 - 4ac$. Then write if the roots of the given equation are real or complex.

1. $5x^2 + 2x + 3 = 0$ _____

2. $x^2 - 10x + 16 = 0$ _____

3. $4x^2 - 5x + 2 = 0$ _____

4. $-x^2 - 6x + 3 = 0$ _____

5. $x^2 + 15x - 20 = 0$ _____

6. $3x^2 - 5x - 1 = 0$ _____

7. $4x^2 - 8x + 12 = 0$ _____

8. $x^2 + x - 1 = 0$ _____

EXAMPLE Using Gauss's definition, $x = \pm i$, and $i = \sqrt{-1}$, substitute i for $\sqrt{-1}$:

$$x = \frac{\pm\sqrt{-16}}{4}$$

Factor $\qquad\qquad x = \frac{\pm(\sqrt{-1})(\sqrt{16})}{4}$

Substitute i for $\sqrt{-1}$ $\qquad x = \frac{\pm i\sqrt{16}}{4}$

$x = \frac{\pm 4i}{4} = \pm i$
The solutions are $x = \pm i$.

Directions Rewrite each number, using i for $\sqrt{-1}$.

9. $\sqrt{-17}$

10. $\sqrt{-23}$

11. $\sqrt{-y}$

12. $\sqrt{-81}$

Directions Use any method to solve these equations. Write complex roots using i for $\sqrt{-1}$.

13. $x^2 + 7x + 3 = 0$ _____

14. $3x^2 + 5x + 11 = 0$ _____

15. $2x^2 + 3x + 4 = 0$ _____

Geometry Connection: Areas

EXAMPLE Write a formula to find the side of a square whose area is 81 cm². Then solve for the side.
Let $x = s$.
$x^2 = 81$
$x = \pm\sqrt{81}$
Take square roots.
$x = \pm 9$
The root $x = -9$ does not make sense for this problem because length cannot be a negative number.
-9 is called an extraneous root.
Solution: $s = 9$ cm

x | $A = 81$ cm²

Directions Find the sides of each square with the given area.

1. 10,000 m² _____

2. 1,600 ft² _____

3. 196 cm² _____

4. 900 in.² _____

5. 625 in.² _____

6. 2,500 yd² _____

EXAMPLE Write a formula to find the sides of a rectangle whose width is 7 cm less than its length, with an area 260 cm². Then solve for l and w.
Let $x = l$ and $x - 7 = w$
$260 = x(x - 7)$
$260 = x^2 - 7x$
$0 = x^2 - 7x - 260$
$0 = (x - 20)(x + 13)$
$x - 20 = 0$ or $x + 13 = 0$
$x = 20$ or $x = -13$

$x - 7$

$A = 260$ cm² x

Solution: $x = 20$, so $l = 20$ cm.
($x = -13$ is an extraneous root.)
$w = x - 7$, $w = 20 - 7 = 13$ cm
Check: Area $= (20$ cm$)(13$ cm$) = 260$ cm²

Directions Find the length and width of the following rectangles.

7. Area $= 88$ yd²; its width is 3 more than its length. _____

8. Area $= 48$ ft²; its width is 8 less than its length. _____

Directions Find the base and height of the following parallelograms.

9. Area $= 117$ in.²; its height is 4 less than its base. _____

10. Area $= 105$ cm²; its height is 8 more than its base. _____

$f(x) = ax^2 + bx + c$, Quadratic Functions

EXAMPLE Given $f(x) = 3x^2 + 4x + 1$:

Find the values for $f(x)$ for $x = 0, 1$, and -1.

$x = 0$: $f(0) = 3(0)^2 + 4(0) + 1 = 1$

independent	(x, y)	dependent
$x = 0$	$(0, 1)$	$f(0) = 1$

$x = 1$: $f(1) = 3(1)^2 + 4(1) + 1 = 8$

independent	(x, y)	dependent
$x = 1$	$(1, 8)$	$f(1) = 8$

$x = -1$: $f(-1) = 3(-1)^2 + 4(-1) + 1 = 0$

independent	(x, y)	dependent
$x = -1$	$(-1, 0)$	$f(-1) = 0$

Directions Find the values of $f(x)$ for the given domain values. Complete a table like the one at the right, listing x and $f(x)$ values for each function.

1. $f(x) = 3x^2 - 4x + 1$
$x = -2, -1, 0, 1, 2$

2. $f(x) = x^2 - 5x + 4$
$x = -1, 0, 1, 2, 3$

3. $f(x) = 2x^2 + 5x + 2$
$x = -2, -1, 0, 1, 2$

4. $f(x) = 4x^2 - 4x + 3$
$x = -1, -\frac{1}{2}, 0, \frac{1}{2}, 1$

5. $f(x) = x^2 + 6x + 5$
$x = -2, -1, 0, 1, 2$

6. $f(x) = x^2 - x + 12$
$x = -2, -1, 0, 1, 2$

7. $f(x) = 4x^2 + 10x + 6$
$x = -1, 0, 1, 2, 3$

8. $f(x) = 3x^2 - 10x + 3$
$x = -2, -1, 0, 1, 2$

9. $f(x) = x^2 - 10x + 8$
$x = -1, -\frac{1}{2}, 0, \frac{1}{2}, 1$

10. $f(x) = 6x^2 + 12x + 6$
$x = -2, -1, 0, 1, 2$

x	$y = f(x)$

Graphing $f(x) = ax^2$ and $f(x) = -ax^2$

EXAMPLE

Graph $f(x) = 3x^2$, domain = all real numbers.

Step 1 Let $x = \pm3, \pm2, \pm1, 0$.
Notice that all the range values are positive except 0 and the graph is above the x-axis.

Step 2 Sketch curve.

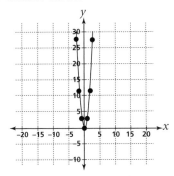

Graph of $f(x) = 3x^2$
Domain = all real numbers
Range = 0 and all positive numbers
The curve is a parabola.

x	$f(x) = 3x^2$
-3	$3(-3)^2 = 27$
3	$3(3)^2 = 27$
-2	$3(-2)^2 = 12$
2	$3(2)^2 = 12$
-1	$3(-1)^2 = 3$
1	$3(1)^2 = 3$
0	$3(0)^2 = 0$

Directions Find seven points for each function. Then sketch the parabola.

1. $f(x) = 5x^2$ _____

2. $f(x) = \frac{1}{9}x^2$ _____

3. $f(x) = -8x^2$ _____

4. $f(x) = -\frac{1}{9}x^2$ _____

5. $f(x) = \frac{1}{8}x^2$ _____

6. $f(x) = -7x^2$ _____

7. $f(x) = -4x^2$ _____

8. $f(x) = -\frac{1}{12}x^2$ _____

9. $f(x) = -\frac{1}{8}x^2$ _____

10. $f(x) = 15x^2$ _____

Graphing $f(x) = ax^2 + c$

EXAMPLE Sketch the graph of $f(x) = 2x^2 - 8$.
Tell if the roots are real or complex.

Solution:

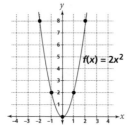

Step 1 Think of $f(x) = 2x^2$.

Step 2 Move curve down by 8 to get $f(x) = 2x^2 - 8$.

Directions Sketch the following parabolas. Write whether the roots are
real or complex numbers.

1. $f(x) = 5x^2 + 3$ _____

2. $f(x) = -x^2 - 15$ _____

3. $f(x) = -6x^2 + 9$ _____

4. $f(x) = 4x^2 + 16$ _____

5. $f(x) = 4x^2 - 5$ _____

6. $f(x) = 6x^2 + 12$ _____

7. $f(x) = 9x^2 - 10$ _____

8. $f(x) = -5x^2 + 5$ _____

9. $f(x) = -4x^2 - 7$ _____

10. $f(x) = 8x^2 + 3$ _____

Directions Sketch the parabolas and answer the questions about each
parabola.

11. Sketch a narrow parabola that spills water and
has a turning point of $(0, -4)$. Will this
parabola have real or complex roots?

_____

12. Sketch a parabola that has a turning point of
$(0, -6)$ and complex roots. What else can you
infer about the parabola?

_____

13. Sketch a wide parabola with real roots and a
turning point of $(0, -10)$. Is the turning point
a minimum or maximum value for $f(x)$?

_____

14. Sketch a parabola with complex roots and a
turning point of $(0, 8)$. Is the turning point a
minimum or maximum value for $f(x)$?

_____

15. Sketch a narrow parabola that holds water
and has a turning point of $(0, 6)$. Will this
parabola have real or complex roots?

_____

Graphing, Using Roots and the Turning Point

EXAMPLE Sketch the graph of $f(x) = x^2 + x - 6$.

Step 1 Find the roots by factoring or using the quadratic formula.

$$x = \frac{-1 \pm \sqrt{1^2 - 4(1)(-6)}}{2(1)}$$

$$x = \frac{-1 \pm \sqrt{1 + 24}}{2}$$

$$x = \frac{-1 \pm \sqrt{25}}{2}$$

$$x = \frac{-1 + 5}{2} \quad \text{or} \quad x = \frac{-1 - 5}{2}$$

$$x = \frac{4}{2} = 2 \quad \text{or} \quad x = \frac{-6}{2} = -3$$

Step 2 Find the x-value of the turning point.

$$x = \frac{-b}{2a} = \frac{-1}{2(1)} = -\frac{1}{2}$$

Step 3 Find the y-value of the turning point. Substitute the x-value into the equation and solve for y.

$$x = -\frac{1}{2}; \ f(-\frac{1}{2}) = (-\frac{1}{2})^2 + (-\frac{1}{2}) - 6$$

$$= \frac{1}{4} - \frac{1}{2} - 6 = -6\frac{1}{4}$$

The turning point is $(-\frac{1}{2}, -6\frac{1}{4})$.

Directions Sketch the graphs, using the function and three points: two roots and the turning point.

1. $f(x) = x^2 + 7x - 8$

2. $f(x) = x^2 - 5x - 6$

3. $f(x) = x^2 + 3x - 10$

4. $f(x) = x^2 + 6x - 16$

5. $f(x) = x^2 - 4x - 5$

EXAMPLE Given the roots $x = -2$ and $x = 6$, sketch the graph.

Step 1 Graph roots.

Step 2 Find midpoint between roots on x-axis: add x-values and divide by 2.

$$x = \frac{-2 + 6}{2} = \frac{4}{2} = 2$$

(x-value of turning point and axis of symmetry)

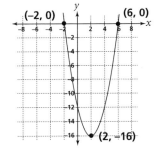

Step 3 Determine $f(x)$. Calculate $f(x)$ for $x = 2$ to find the y-value of the turning point. Roots of $x = -2$ and $x = 6$ mean factors are $(x + 2)$ and $(x - 6)$.

$$f(x) = (x + 2)(x - 6)$$
$$= x^2 - 4x - 12$$
$$f(2) = (2)^2 - 4(2) - 12$$
$$= 4 - 8 - 12$$
$$= -16$$

The turning point is $(2, -16)$.

Directions Sketch the graphs, using the given roots to determine the function and the turning point.

6. $x = -3, x = 1$

7. $x = -5, x = 3$

8. $x = -2, x = 4$

9. $x = -8, x = -6$

10. $x = 3, x = 7$

Reading Quadratic Graphs

Given $f(x) = ax^2 + bx + c$, $x = \dfrac{-b \pm \sqrt{b^2 - 4ac}}{2a}$

Which graph represents the described $f(x)$?

$f(x)$ has a zero radicand.
Solution: If $f(x)$ has a zero radicand, $f(x)$
has two equal roots; graph B
represents the function.

$f(x)$ has a negative radicand.
Solution: If $f(x)$ has a negative radicand,
$f(x)$ has complex roots; graph C
represents the function.

$f(x)$ has a positive radicand.
Solution: If $f(x)$ has a positive radicand,
$f(x)$ has real roots; graph F
represents the function.

A   B

C 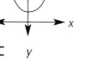   D

E   F

Directions Read the graphs and determine whether the parabola is a
function. Write *function* or *not a function*.

1. 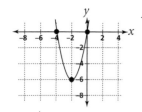 _____

2. 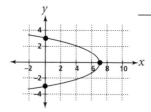 _____

Directions Read the graph. Circle the function that represents the graph.

3. A $f(x) = -6x^2$
    B $f(x) = 6x^2$

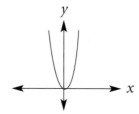

4. A $f(x) = -3x^2 - 8$
    B $f(x) = -3x^2 + 8$

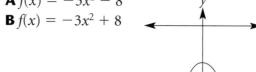

Directions Read the graph. Decide if the roots are real or complex.
Write *real* or *complex*.

5. 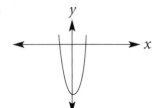 _____

Parabolas and Straight Lines

EXAMPLE

Find the common solutions to
$y = f(x) = x^2 + 3$ and $y = 3x + 1$.

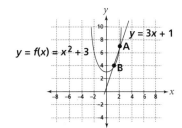

Step 1 Equate y-values.
Equate $y = x^2 + 3$ and $y = 3x + 1$.
$x^2 + 3 = 3x + 1$
$x^2 = 3x - 2$
$0 = x^2 - 3x + 2$

Step 2 Solve for x.
$0 = x^2 - 3x + 2$
$0 = (x - 2)(x - 1)$
$x - 2 = 0$ or $x - 1 = 0$
$x = 2$ or $x = 1$

Step 3 Substitute in either function.
$x = 2$, $y = 3x + 1 \rightarrow y = 3(2) + 1 = 7$
Point A is $(2, 7)$.
$x = 1$, $y = 3(1) + 1 = 4$
Point B is $(1, 4)$.

Directions Find the common solutions. Give the coordinates of points
A and B.

1. $y = f(x) = 2x^2$
$y = 8$

2. $y = f(x) = \frac{1}{3}x^2$
$y = x + 6$

3. $y = f(x) = -4x^2$
$y = 8x - 12$

EXAMPLE

Use algebra to show that there are no common solutions to
$y = f(x) = x^2$ and $y = x - 4$.

Step 1 Equate y-values.
Equate $y = x^2$ and $y = x - 4$.
$x^2 = x - 4$
$x^2 - x + 4 = 0$

Step 2 Solve for x.

$x^2 - x + 4 = 0$

$x = \dfrac{1 \pm \sqrt{-15}}{2}$

$x = \dfrac{1 \pm i\sqrt{15}}{2}$

Step 3 $x = \dfrac{1 \pm i\sqrt{15}}{2}$

indicates the system of equations has complex
roots. The graphs of the functions do not
intersect.

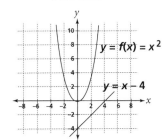

Directions Use algebra to show that there are no common solutions.

4. $y = f(x) = x^2 - 3$
$y = x - 8$

5. $y = f(x) = x^2$
$y = -4$

The Straight Lines

EXAMPLE Check if the system of linear equations has a common solution.
If it does, find the common solution.

Step 1 Compare the slopes of each line.
If they are not equal then they have a common solution.
$y = 3x + 7$ $m = 3$
$y = x - 9$ $m = 1$
The slopes are not equal. Therefore, the system has a common solution.

Step 2 Elimination Method
Equate y from the equations.
Rewrite $y = 3x + 7$ as $y - 3x = 7$
Rewrite $y = x - 9$ as $y - x = -9$
Subtract to eliminate y. $y - 3x = 7$
$\quad y - x = -9$
$ y - y - 3x - (-x) = 7 - (-9)$
$ -2x = 16$
$ x = -8$

Step 3 Use this value of x to find the corresponding value of y.
$x = -8, y = 3x + 7 \to y = 3(-8) + 7 = -17$
$x = -8, y = x - 9 \to y = (-8) - 9 = -17$
Common solution: $(-8, -17)$

Directions Determine whether the system has a common solution.
Write *yes* or *no*.

1. $y = 2x + 4$ _____
$\ y = 4x - 2$

2. $3y + x = 6$ _____
$\ y = 3x$

3. $2x + 8 = y$ _____
$\ y = 2x - 6$

4. $3x - 6y = 4$ _____
$\ 5x = 3y - 6$

5. $y + 12 = 3x$ _____
$\ y = 3x - 6$

6. $9x + 3y = 6$ _____
$\ 8y = 16x - 2$

Directions Find the common solution for each system of equations.

7. $y = 4x - 2$ _____
$\ y = 2x + 3$

8. $4y + 4x = 8$ _____
$\ y + 2x = 4$

9. $2y + 4x = 12$ _____
$\ 3x + y = 5$

10. $5x + 6 = y$ _____
$\ 4x - 7 = y$

Word Problems and Linear Equations

EXAMPLE   The sum of two numbers is 26, and their difference is 8. What are the numbers?

Solution: Let x = one number, y = the other number

$x + y = 26$ Sum is 26.

$x - y = 8$ Difference is 8.

Add the equations:

$$x + y = 26$$
$$x - y = 8$$
$$2x - 0 = 34$$
$$x = 17$$

Substitute: $x + y = 26 \rightarrow 17 + y = 26 \rightarrow y = 9$

Common solution is (17, 9).

Check: $17 + 9 = 26$, $17 - 9 = 8$ True.

Directions Solve.

1. The sum of two numbers is 34. The difference of the two numbers is 12. What are the numbers?

_____

2. The sum of two numbers is 83. The difference of the two numbers is 17. What are the numbers?

_____

3. The sum of two numbers is 62. The difference of the two numbers is 18. What are the numbers?

_____

4. The sum of two numbers is 57. The difference of the two numbers is 11. What are the numbers?

_____

5. The sum of two numbers is 88. The difference of the two numbers is 32. What are the numbers?

_____

6. You have 27 coins consisting of pennies and nickels. The coins total $0.83. How many coins are pennies? How many are nickels?

_____

7. You have 31 coins consisting of nickels and dimes. The coins total $2.25. How many coins are nickels? How many are dimes?

_____

8. You have 59 coins consisting of pennies and nickels. The coins total $2.87. How many coins are pennies? How many are nickels?

_____

9. You have 67 coins consisting of dimes and nickels. The coins total $3.95. How many coins are dimes? How many are nickels?

_____

10. You have 24 coins consisting of dimes and quarters. The coins total $3.15. How many coins are dimes? How many are quarters?

_____

Geometry Connection: Axis of Symmetry

EXAMPLES   Matching points must be equidistant from the axis of symmetry.

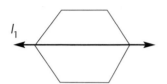   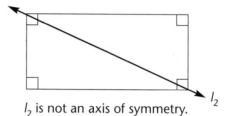

l_1 is an axis of symmetry. l_2 is not an axis of symmetry.

Directions Which is an axis of symmetry for the given figure?
Write l_1 or l_2.

1. _____

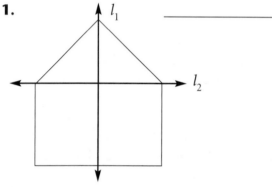

4. _____

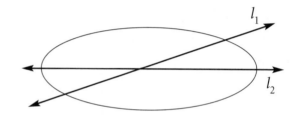

2. _____

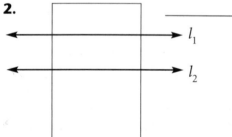

5.

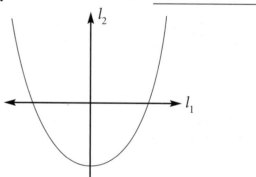

3. _____

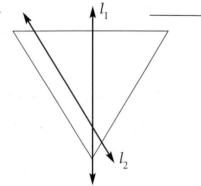

Definitions, Addition

EXAMPLE   Add $5x^3 - 9x^2y + 7xy^2 - 2x + 15$ and $4x^2y^2 - x^2y - 8xy^2 + 5x - 10$.

Group like terms, then add.

$$
\begin{array}{llllll}
5x^3 & & -\ 9x^2y & +\ 7xy^2 & -\ 2x & +\ 15 \\
& +\ 4x^2y^2 & -\ x^2y & -\ 8xy^2 & +\ 5x & -\ 10 \\
\hline
5x^3 & +\ 4x^2y^2 & -\ 10x^2y & -\ xy^2 & +\ 3x & +\ 5
\end{array}
$$

Directions Add the expressions.

1. $x^4y^2 + 6x^2y - 3xy^2$ and $3x^3y^2 - 8x^2y + xy^2 - 10x$

_____

2. $3x^3y^2 + 8x^2y - 12xy + 16x - 10$ and $4x^3y^2 - 7x^2y + 6xy + 4y^2 + 4$

_____

3. $9x^4y^3 + 3x^3y^2 - 7x^2y - 6y^3 + 6y^2 - 18$ and $12x^3y^2 - 14x^2y + 7y^2 - 11$

_____

4. $3x^4y^2 + 6x^3y^2 - 7x^2y^2 - 10xy^2 - 14y + 17$ and $-7x^3y^2 + 7x^2y^2 + 19xy^2 - y - 4$

_____

5. $10x^4y^3 - 7x^3y^3 + 16x^2y - 8xy^3 - 7xy + 2$ and $4x^3y^3 - 8x^2y - 8xy^3 - 6xy - 12$

_____

Directions: Find the difference.

6. Subtract $3x^3y^2 - 8x^2y + xy^2 - 10x$ from $x^4y^2 + 6x^2y - 3xy^2$.

_____

7. Subtract $4x^3y^2 - 7x^2y + 6xy + 4y^2 + 4$ from $3x^3y^2 + 8x^2y - 12xy + 16x - 10$.

_____

8. Subtract $12x^3y^2 - 14x^2y + 7y^2 - 11$ from $9x^4y^3 + 3x^3y^2 - 7x^2y - 6y^3 + 6y^2 - 18$.

_____

9. Subtract $-7x^3y^2 + 7x^2y^2 + 19xy^2 - y - 4$ from $3x^4y^2 + 6x^3y^2 - 7x^2y^2 - 10xy^2 - 14y + 17$.

_____

10. Subtract $4x^3y^3 - 8x^2y - 8xy^3 - 6xy - 12$ from $10x^4y^3 - 7x^3y^3 + 16x^2y - 8xy^3 - 7xy + 2$.

_____

Products: $(a + b)^2$, $(a - b)^2$, $(a + b)^3$, $(a - b)^3$

EXAMPLE Find $(2x - 4y)^2$.
Model method: $(a + b)^2 = a^2 + 2ab + b^2$
Let $a = 2x$, $b = -4y$.
$(2x - 4y)^2 = (2x)^2 + 2(2x)(-4y) + (-4y)^2$
$\qquad\qquad = 4x^2 - 16xy + 16y^2$

Directions Write the expressions in expanded form.

1. $(2x + 6)^2$ _____

2. $(3x + 4)^2$ _____

3. $(5x - 1)^2$ _____

4. $(3x + 2y)^2$ _____

5. $(4m + 4n)^2$ _____

6. $(3a - 4b)^2$ _____

7. $(6x - 6y)^2$ _____

8. $(q + 5r)^2$ _____

9. $(4t - 3v)^2$ _____

10. $(8x - y)^2$ _____

EXAMPLE Find $(3x - y)^3$.

Factor method:
$(3x - y)^3 = (3x - y)(3x - y)^2$
$\qquad\quad = (3x - y)(9x^2 - 6xy + y^2)$
$\qquad\quad = 3x(9x^2 - 6xy + y^2) - y(9x^2 - 6xy + y^2)$
$\qquad\quad = 27x^3 - 18x^2y + 3xy^2 - 9x^2y + 6xy^2 - y^3$
$\qquad\quad = 27x^3 - 27x^2y + 9xy^2 - y^3$

Model method: $(a + b)^3 = a^3 + 3a^2b + 3ab^2 + b^3$
Let $a = 3x$, $b = -y$.
$(3x - y)^3 = (3x)^3 + 3(3x)^2(-y) + 3(3x)(-y)^2 + (-y)^3$
$\qquad\quad = 27x^3 - 27x^2y + 9xy^2 - y^3$

Directions Write the expressions in expanded form.

11. $(y + z)^3$ _____

12. $(3x + 4)^3$ _____

13. $(2x - y)^3$ _____

14. $(3x + 2y)^3$ _____

15. $(5x - 3y)^3$ _____

Factoring $a^2 - b^2$, $a^3 + b^3$, and $a^3 - b^3$

EXAMPLES   Find the factors of $4x^2 - 4y^2$.
Solution: Use the model $a^2 - b^2 = (a + b)(a - b)$.
Let $a = 2x$, $b = 2y$; then $2x^2 - 2y^2 = (2x + 2y)(2x - 2y)$.

Find the factors of $y^3 + z^3$.
Solution: Use the model $a^3 + b^3 = (a + b)(a^2 - ab + b^2)$.
Let $a = y$, $b = z$; then $y^3 + z^3 = (y + z)(y^2 - yz + z^2)$.

Factor $x^3 - 8$.
Solution: Use the model $a^3 - b^3 = (a - b)(a^2 + ab + b^2)$.
Let $a = x$, $b = 2$; then $x^3 - 8 = (x - 2)(x^2 + 2x + 4)$.

Directions Find the factors. Use a model.

1. $m^2 - n^2$ _____

2. $9x^2 - y^2$ _____

3. $16x^2 - 4y^2$ _____

4. $100x^2 - 25y^2$ _____

5. $49m^2 - 64n^2$ _____

6. $8x^3 + y^3$ _____

7. $p^3 + r^3$ _____

8. $x^3 + 27y^3$ _____

9. $8x^3 + 64y^3$ _____

10. $125s^3 + 8t^3$ _____

11. $t^3 - w^3$ _____

12. $8x^3 - 8y^3$ _____

13. $64a^3 - 8$ _____

14. $27 - b^3$ _____

15. $216a^3 - 125b^3$ _____

Multiplication of Polynomials

EXAMPLES Multiply the polynomials. Simplify and write the answer alphabetically and in descending order of the power of the terms.

$(x + 3y)(x^3 - 4x + 8)$
$= x(x^3 - 4x + 8) + 3y(x^3 - 4x + 8)$
$= x^4 - 4x^2 + 8x + 3x^3y - 12xy + 24y$
$= x^4 + 3x^3y - 4x^2 + 8x - 12xy + 24y$

$(x - y)^2(4x + y)^2$
$= (x^2 - 2xy + y^2)(16x^2 + 8xy + y^2)$
$= x^2(16x^2 + 8xy + y^2) - 2xy(16x^2 + 8xy + y^2) + y^2(16x^2 + 8xy + y^2)$
$= 16x^4 + 8x^3y + x^2y^2 - 32x^3y - 16x^2y^2 - 2xy^3 + 16x^2y^2 + 8xy^3 + y^4$
$= 16x^4 - 24x^3y + x^2y^2 + 6xy^3 + y^4$

Directions Multiply. Write the answer alphabetically in descending order of the power of the terms.

1. $(x^2 + 3)(x^3 + 2x)$ _____

2. $(2x - 4y)(x^3 + x)$ _____

3. $(5x^2 - 4)(x^2 + 15)$ _____

4. $(x^3 + 7x^2 - 2)(x - y)$ _____

5. $(8x^2 + y)(x - 2y + 7y^2)$ _____

6. $(3x^3 + y)(x^2 - 2x + 4y + 1)$ _____

7. $(4x^2 - 4)(6y^2 - 2x + 3)$ _____

8. $(x + 3)(x^2 - xy + y^2)$ _____

9. $(3x + 2y)(x - 3y + 8y^2)$ _____

10. $(x^2 - 7)(x^2 + 2xy^2 - 3)$ _____

11. $(x - 4y + 8z)(4x + 9y - 7z)$ _____

12. $(x^3 + 2x^2y + 2y)(x^2 - 3y + 2)$ _____

13. $(3x - y)(x^2 + 3xy - 4)$ _____

14. $(7x + 2y - 8z)(2x - 4z)$ _____

15. $(2x^2 - 4x)(x + 3y^2 - 7y)$ _____

16. $(4x^3 - 2y^2 - 12)(2x + 3y^2)$ _____

17. $(x^2 + 7xy - 4y)(x^2 - 5xy)$ _____

18. $(x - 3y)^2(5x + 2y)$ _____

19. $(3x + 5)^2(2x + y)$ _____

20. $(4x - y)^2(x - y)^2$ _____

Division of Polynomials; Rational Expressions

EXAMPLES   Find the quotient of $(6x^3 \div 2x^2)$.

$6x^3 \div 2x^2 = \frac{6x^3}{2x^2} = \frac{(2)(3)(x)(x)(x)}{(2)(x)(x)} = 3x$

Find the quotient of $(x^3 - y^3) \div (x - y)$.

Factor the numerator; then look for common factors.

$\frac{(x - y)(x^2 + xy + y^2)}{(x - y)} = x^2 + xy + y^2$

Directions Divide.

1. $7x^3 \div x$ _____

2. $(4x^2 - x) \div x$ _____

3. $(15x^4 + 3x^3) \div 3x$ _____

4. $(18x^5 - 6x^2) \div 2x^2$ _____

5. $(x + y)^5 \div (x + y)^3$ _____

6. $(6x - 4)^6 \div (6x - 4)^3$ _____

7. $(x^2 + 4xy + 4y^2) \div (x + 2y)$ _____

8. $(4x^2 - 20x + 25) \div (2x - 5)$ _____

9. $(9x^2 + 24xy + 16y^2) \div (3x + 4y)$ _____

10. $(x^3 + y^3) \div (x + y)$ _____

11. $(8x^3 - 27) \div (2x - 3)$ _____

12. $(64x^3 + y^3) \div (4x + y)$ _____

13. $(16x^2 - 4y^2) \div (4x + 2y)$ _____

14. $(25 - 100y^2) \div (5 - 10y)$ _____

15. $(8x^3 + 8y^3) \div (4x^2 - 4xy + 4y^2)$ _____

Long Division of Polynomials

EXAMPLE   Divide $2a^3 + 4a^2b + 4ab^2 + 2b^3$ by $a + b$.

$$
\begin{array}{r}
2a^2 + \ 2ab + 2b^2 \\
(a+b) \ \overline{)\ 2a^3 + 4a^2b + 4ab^2 + 2b^3} \\
\underline{2a^3 + 2a^2b} \\
0 + 2a^2b \\
\underline{2a^2b + 2ab^2} \\
0 + 2ab^2 \\
\underline{2ab^2 + 2b^3} \\
0 + \ 0
\end{array}
$$

Rules for Dividing Polynomials

1. Arrange dividend and divisor in order of descending powers of the same variable. If necessary, supply any missing powers by writing (0)(the missing power).

2. Divide the first term of the dividend by the first term of the divisor. The result is the first term of the quotient.

3. Multiply the entire divisor by this term of the quotient. Subtract the product from the dividend.

4. Treat this result as a new dividend and repeat steps 1–3 until the remainder is 0 or until the power of the remainder is less than the highest power of the divisor.

Directions   Use long division to find the quotient.

1. $(a^2 - 8a + 16) \div (a - 4)$ _____

2. $(x^2 - x - 12) \div (x - 4)$ _____

3. $(8x^2 + 2x - 3) \div (2x - 1)$ _____

4. $(9x^2 + 30x + 25) \div (3x + 5)$ _____

5. $(4x^2 - 25) \div (2x + 5)$ _____

6. $(x^3 + x^2 + 3x + 3) \div (x + 1)$ _____

7. $(x^6 + 2x^4 - 5x^2 - 10) \div (x^2 + 2)$ _____

8. $(12x^2 + x - 10) \div (4x + 3)$ _____

9. $(2x^5 + 6x^3 + 2x^2 + 4) \div (x^2 + 3)$ _____

10. $(x^3 + y^3) \div (x + y)$ _____

Complex Fractions

EXAMPLE Simplify $\dfrac{\frac{1}{x}}{\frac{1}{x^3}}$.

$$\frac{\frac{1}{x}}{\frac{1}{x^3}} = \frac{(\frac{1}{x})(\frac{x^3}{1})}{(\frac{1}{x^3})(\frac{x^3}{1})} = \frac{\frac{x^3}{x}}{1} = x^2$$

Directions Simplify the complex fractions. Write the answers in simplest form.

1. $\dfrac{\frac{1}{x^2}}{\frac{1}{x^4}}$ _____

2. $\dfrac{\frac{1}{y}}{\frac{1}{y^4}}$ _____

3. $\dfrac{\frac{1}{2}}{\frac{1}{3}}$ _____

4. $\dfrac{\frac{1}{4}}{\frac{2}{3}}$ _____

5. $\dfrac{\frac{5}{6}}{\frac{3}{10}}$ _____

6. $\dfrac{4}{\frac{3}{5}}$ _____

7. $\dfrac{\frac{5}{6}}{2}$ _____

8. $\dfrac{x}{\frac{1}{x^2}}$ _____

9. $\dfrac{\frac{x}{5}}{x^3}$ _____

10. $\dfrac{\frac{3}{x}}{\frac{x^5}{2}}$ _____

11. $\dfrac{\frac{z^2}{3}}{\frac{1}{z^3}}$ _____

12. $\dfrac{\frac{3}{m^2}}{\frac{m^4}{6}}$ _____

13. $\dfrac{t}{\frac{3}{t^3}}$ _____

14. $\dfrac{\frac{2}{m}}{\frac{m^3}{5}}$ _____

15. $\dfrac{\frac{4a}{b}}{\frac{b^3}{a^2}}$ _____

16. $\dfrac{\frac{8x^2}{y^3}}{\frac{10x^5}{y}}$ _____

17. $\dfrac{\frac{x}{3}}{2x^4}$ _____

18. $\dfrac{\frac{7y}{3}}{y^3}$ _____

19. $\dfrac{\frac{16m^3}{n^2}}{4m^2n}$ _____

20. $\dfrac{\frac{15x^3y^2}{z}}{\frac{3y^3z}{x^2}}$ _____

Geometry Connection: Perimeter Formulas

EXAMPLE   Use the variables for the sides of the trapezoid to write
a formula for the perimeter p. Simplify the algebra.

$p = h + h + a + b$

$p = 2h + a + b$

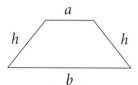

Directions   Use the letters of the given geometric figures to write a
formula for each figure's perimeter. Let p = perimeter.
Write in simplest form.

1.

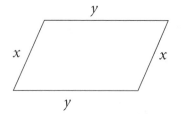

_____

2.

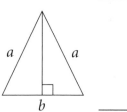

_____

3.

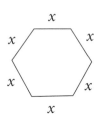

_____

4.

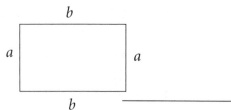

_____

5.

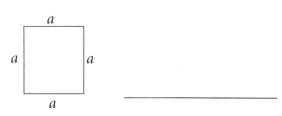

_____

6.

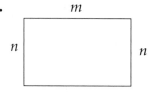

_____

7.

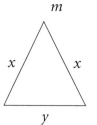

_____

8.

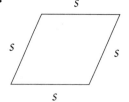

_____

9.

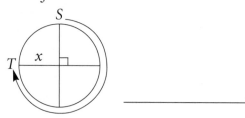

_____

10.

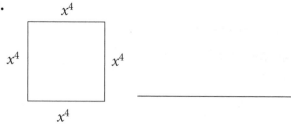

_____

Simplifying Rational Expressions

EXAMPLE   Simplify $\frac{x^3y^4z^5}{xy^3z^3}$ Factor: $\frac{x\,x\,x\,y\,y\,y\,y\,z\,z\,z\,z\,z}{x\,y\,y\,y\,z\,z\,z}$

Find common factor: xy^3z^3

Divide by common factor: $\frac{x\,x\,x\,\cancel{x}\,\cancel{x}\,\cancel{x}\,\cancel{y}\,y\,\cancel{z}\,\cancel{z}\,\cancel{z}\,z\,z}{\cancel{x}\,\cancel{y}\,\cancel{y}\,\cancel{y}\,\cancel{z}\,\cancel{z}\,\cancel{z}} = \frac{x^3y^4z^5}{xy^3z^3} = x^2yz^2$

Directions   Simplify each rational expression. If there are no common factors, write *lowest terms*.

1. $\frac{x^2y^2z^2}{xyz}$ _____

2. $\frac{a^3b^4c^5}{a^2b^5c^3}$ _____

3. $\frac{a^2xy}{b^2xy}$ _____

4. $\frac{a^2x^2z}{a^2b^2z}$ _____

5. $\frac{a^2x}{b^2y}$ _____

6. $\frac{3b^2cd^5}{9b^5cd^2}$ _____

7. $\frac{mn^2}{m^2n^2}$ _____

8. $\frac{r^2st^2}{rst^2}$ _____

9. $\frac{a^2x^2b}{axb}$ _____

10. $\frac{5k^5mn}{7k^4m^3n^3}$ _____

EXAMPLE $\frac{a^2 - 2ab + b^2}{a - b}$ Factor: $\frac{(a - b)(a - b)}{(a - b)}$

Find common factor: $(a - b)$

Divide by common factor: $\frac{\cancel{(a - b)}(a - b)}{\cancel{(a - b)}}$

$\frac{a^2 - 2ab + b^2}{a - b} = (a - b)$

Directions   Simplify each rational expression. If there are no common factors, write *lowest terms*.

11. $\frac{(a + b)^2}{(a + b)}$ _____

12. $\frac{(a + b)}{(a^2 - b^2)}$ _____

13. $\frac{(x + y)^3}{(x^2 - y^2)}$ _____

14. $\frac{(a^2 + 2ab + b^2)}{(a + b)^2}$ _____

15. $\frac{(a^3 + 2a^2b + ab^2)}{(a^2 + ab)}$ _____

16. $\frac{(ax + ay + bx + by)}{(a + b)(x + y)}$ _____

17. $\frac{(a - b)(a + b)^2}{(a^2 - b^2)}$ _____

18. $\frac{(m - n)^3}{m^2 - 2mn + n^2}$ _____

19. $\frac{(m^3 + n^3)}{(x + y)}$ _____

20. $\frac{(m^3 + n^3)}{(m + n)}$ _____

Adding and Subtracting Rational Expressions

EXAMPLE Add: $\frac{(3a + b)}{(a + b)} + \frac{(4a + 2b)}{(a + b)^2}$

Multiply to create a common denominator.

$$[\frac{(3a + b)}{(a + b)}][\frac{(a + b)}{(a + b)}] + \frac{(4a + 2b)}{(a + b)^2}$$

Add numerators. $= \frac{(3a + b)(a + b) + (4a + 2b)}{(a + b)^2}$

Simplify. $= \frac{(3a^2 + 4a + 4ab + b^2 + 2b)}{(a + b)^2}$

Directions Add. Express your answer in lowest terms.

1. $\frac{x^2y}{a} + \frac{2xy}{a}$ _____

2. $\frac{a^2bc}{ef} + \frac{abc}{ef}$ _____

3. $\frac{a^2b^2}{c} + \frac{b^2d^2}{c^2}$ _____

4. $\frac{(a + b)}{(a^2 - b^2)} + \frac{(a - b)}{(a + b)}$ _____

5. $\frac{(x - y)}{(x^2 - y^2)} + \frac{(x + y)}{(x - y)}$ _____

6. $\frac{m^2n^2}{rt^2} + \frac{m^3n^3}{rt^2}$ _____

7. $\frac{cd^2}{xy} + \frac{cd^2}{x^2y^2}$ _____

8. $\frac{(a + b)^2}{(a - b)} + \frac{(a - b)^2}{(a^2 - b^2)}$ _____

9. $\frac{16xy}{z^3} + \frac{64x^2y^2}{z^3}$ _____

10. $\frac{6x^2y^3z}{a^2} + \frac{4x^2y^3z}{a}$ _____

EXAMPLE Subtract: $\frac{(3a + b)}{(a + b)} - \frac{(4a + 2b)}{(a + b)^2}$

Multiply to create a common denominator.

$$[\frac{(3a + b)}{(a + b)}][\frac{(a + b)}{(a + b)}] - \frac{(4a + 2b)}{(a + b)^2}$$

Subtract numerators. $= \frac{[(3a + b)(a + b) - (4a + 2b)]}{(a + b)^2}$

Simplify. $= \frac{(3a^2 - 4a + 4ab + b^2 - 2b)}{(a + b)^2}$

Directions Subtract. Express your answer in lowest terms.

11. $\frac{a^2bc}{ef} - \frac{abc}{ef}$ _____

12. $\frac{a^2b^2}{c} - \frac{b^2d^2}{c^2}$ _____

13. $\frac{x^2y}{a} - \frac{2xy}{a}$ _____

14. $\frac{(x - y)}{(x^2 - y^2)} - \frac{(x + y)}{(x - y)}$ _____

15. $\frac{(a + b)}{(a^2 - b^2)} - \frac{(a - b)}{(a + b)}$ _____

16. $\frac{cd^2}{xy} - \frac{cd^2}{x^2y^2}$ _____

17. $\frac{m^2n^2}{rt^2} - \frac{m^3n^3}{rt^2}$ _____

18. $\frac{64x^2y^2}{z^3} - \frac{16xy}{z^3}$ _____

19. $\frac{6x^2y^3z}{a^3} - \frac{4x^2y^3z}{a}$ _____

20. $\frac{(a + b)^2}{(a - b)} - \frac{(a - b)^2}{(a^2 - b^2)}$ _____

Multiplying Rational Expressions

EXAMPLE $[\frac{a^2 - 2ab + b^2}{(a + b)}][\frac{(a + b)}{(a - b)}]$

Multiply numerators, then multiply denominators.

$$\frac{(a^2 - 2ab + b^2)(a + b)}{(a + b)(a - b)}$$

Factor and simplify. $= \frac{(a - b)(a - b)(a + b)}{(a + b)(a - b)} = (a - b)$

Directions Multiply. Give your answer in lowest terms.

1. $(\frac{x^2}{3y^3})(\frac{x^3}{4y^2})$ _____

2. $[\frac{(x + y)}{y^2}][\frac{(x - y)}{x^2}]$ _____

3. $(\frac{4a^3}{b^2})(\frac{4b^3}{a^2})$ _____

4. $[\frac{(a + b)}{(a^2 - b^2)}][\frac{(a + b)}{(a^2 + b^2)}]$ _____

5. $[\frac{(x + 2)}{4y}][\frac{3y}{(x^2 - 4)}]$ _____

6. $[\frac{(a + b)}{2b}][\frac{(a - b)}{(a + b)}]$ _____

7. $[\frac{2(a - b)}{(a + b)}][\frac{4(a + b)}{(a - b)}]$ _____

8. $[\frac{6(a^2 + b^2)}{5(a + b)^2}][\frac{3(a + b)}{7(a^2 - b^2)}]$ _____

9. $[\frac{(x^2 + 2xy + y^2)}{(x + y)}][\frac{(x - y)^2}{(x + y)}]$ _____

10. $[\frac{(x^2 + 4)}{(x^2 + 2xy + y^2)}][\frac{(x^2 - 4)}{(x^2 - 2xy + y^2)}]$ _____

11. $[\frac{(a^2 + 2ab + b^2)}{(a^2 - b^2)}][\frac{(a - b)}{(a^2 + b^2)}]$ _____

12. $[\frac{(x^2 - xy + y^2)}{(x + y)}][\frac{(x + y)}{(x - y)}]$ _____

13. $[\frac{(x - y)}{(x + y)}][\frac{(x^2 + xy + y^2)}{(x^2 + 2xy + y^2)}]$ _____

14. $[\frac{xy(a + b)}{(a - b)}][\frac{xy(a - b)}{(a + b)}]$ _____

15. $[\frac{(3(a + 2)}{(a^2 + 4)}][\frac{3(a - 2)}{(a^2 - 4)}]$ _____

Dividing Rational Expressions

EXAMPLE
$$\frac{(x^2 - y^2)}{xy} \div \frac{(x + y)}{x}$$

Multiply by the reciprocal of $\frac{(x + y)}{x}$: $\frac{x}{(x + y)}$.

$$[\frac{x^2 - y^2}{xy}][\frac{x}{(x + y)}] = \frac{(x + y)(x - y)x}{xy(x + y)}$$

Factor and simplify.
$$= \frac{(x + y)(x - y)x}{xy(x + y)} = \frac{(x - y)}{y}$$

Directions Divide. Give your answer in lowest terms.

1. $\frac{x^2}{3y^3} \div \frac{x^3}{4y^2}$ _____

2. $\frac{(x + y)}{y^2} \div \frac{(x - y)}{x^2}$ _____

3. $\frac{4a^3}{b^2} \div \frac{4b^3}{a^2}$ _____

4. $\frac{(a + b)}{(a^2 - b^2)} \div \frac{(a + b)}{(a^2 + b^2)}$ _____

5. $\frac{(x + 2)}{4y} \div \frac{3y}{(x^2 - 4)}$ _____

6. $\frac{(a + b)}{2b} \div \frac{(a - b)}{(a + b)}$ _____

7. $\frac{2(a - b)}{(a + b)} \div \frac{4(a + b)}{(a - b)}$ _____

8. $\frac{6(a^2 + b^2)}{5(a + b)^2} \div \frac{3(a + b)}{7(a^2 - b^2)}$ _____

9. $\frac{(x^2 + 2xy + y^2)}{(x + y)} \div \frac{(x - y)^2}{(x + y)}$ _____

10. $\frac{(x^2 + 4)}{(x^2 + 2xy + y^2)} \div \frac{(x^2 - 2xy + y^2)}{(x^2 - 4)}$ _____

11. $\frac{(a^2 + 2ab + b^2)}{(a^2 - b^2)} \div \frac{(a - b)}{(a^2 + b^2)}$ _____

12. $\frac{(x^2 - xy + y^2)}{(x + y)} \div \frac{(x - y)}{(x + y)}$ _____

13. $\frac{(x - y)}{(x + y)} \div \frac{(x^2 + 2xy + y^2)}{(x^2 + xy + y^2)}$ _____

14. $\frac{xy(a + b)}{(a - b)} \div \frac{xy(a - b)}{(a + b)}$ _____

15. $\frac{3(a + 2)}{(a^2 + 4)} \div \frac{3(a - 2)}{(a^2 - 4)}$ _____

Geometry Connection: Similar Figures

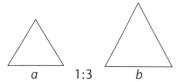

EXAMPLE

The triangles are similar.
Their sides have the proportions 1:3.

Given $\frac{a}{b} = \frac{1}{3} = \frac{\text{smaller}}{\text{larger}}$

If $b = 30$, how long is a?

Solution: x is unknown. Let $\frac{x}{b} = \frac{1}{3} = \frac{\text{smaller}}{\text{larger}}$

Solve for x. $\frac{x}{30} = \frac{1}{3}$

Multiply by 30. $x = (30)(\frac{1}{3})$

$x = \frac{30}{3} = 10$

Directions   Find the unknown lengths. The given figures are similar.

a b

Given $\frac{a}{b} = \frac{1}{5}$

1. If $b = 30$, what is a?   _____

2. If $a = 10$, what is b?   _____

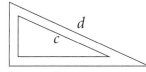

Given $\frac{c}{d} = \frac{2}{7}$

3. If $c = 30$, what is d?   _____

4. If $d = 35$, what is c?   _____

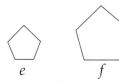

e f

Given $\frac{e}{f} = \frac{1}{4}$

5. If $f = 100$, what is e?   _____

6. If the perimeter of the larger
figure is 20, what is the perimeter
of the smaller figure?   _____

g h

Given $\frac{g}{h} = \frac{3}{8}$

7. If $h = 6$, what is g?   _____

8. If the perimeter of the smaller
figure is 24, what is the perimeter
of the larger figure?   _____

Given $\frac{l}{m} = \frac{1}{3}$

9. If the radius of $l = 6$, what is
the radius of m?   _____

10. If the diameter of the larger
figure is 39, what is the diameter
of the smaller figure?   _____

Positive Powers—Basic Rules

(**EXAMPLES**) 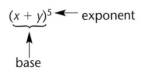 $(x + y)^5$ ← exponent

base

Find the product of $(a + b)^6 \cdot (a + b)^4$.
Make sure each base is the same.
Add exponents.
$(a + b)^6 \cdot (a + b)^4 = (a + b)^{(6 + 4)} = (a + b)^{10}$

Find the quotient of $(a + b)^6 \div (a + b)^4$.
Make sure each base is the same.
Subtract exponents.
$(a + b)^6 \div (a + b)^4 = (a + b)^{(6 - 4)} = (a + b)^2$

Directions Find the products and quotients.

1. $6^5 \cdot 6^2$ _____

2. $(m^5)(m)$ _____

3. $(a^3)(b^6)$ _____

4. $2^5 \div 2^2$ _____

5. $d^6 \div d^2$ _____

6. $a^5 \div x^5$ _____

7. $m^6 \cdot m^6$ _____

8. $(x + y)^2 \cdot (x + y)^4$ _____

9. $\frac{(xy)^4}{(xy)^3}$ _____

10. $(a + b)^2 \cdot (a + b)^2$ _____

11. $(x + y)^4 \div (x + y)$ _____

12. $(c + d)^6 \cdot (a + b)^4$ _____

13. $d^6 \div d^6$ _____

14. $\frac{(a + b)^3}{(a + b)}$ _____

15. $(y + 3)^{10} \cdot \frac{(x - 4)^4}{(y + 3)(x - 4)^2}$ _____

Negative Exponents

EXAMPLE $a^9 \div a^{12} = a^{(9-12)} = a^{-3}$. Remember that $x^{-m} = \frac{1}{x^m}$.

$a^{-3} = \frac{1}{a^3}$

Directions Divide. Give your answer using negative exponents.
Then rewrite your answer using positive exponents.

1. $\frac{6^5}{6^9}$ _____

2. $m^5 \div m^6$ _____

3. $b^3 \div b^6$ _____

4. $2^5 \div 2^7$ _____

5. $d^4 \div d^8$ _____

6. $a^5 \div a^6$ _____

7. $\frac{n^4 m^6}{n^7 m^8}$ _____

8. $\frac{(x+y)^2}{(x+y)^4}$ _____

9. $xy^4 \div xy^7$ _____

10. $\frac{(a+b)^4}{(a+b)^8}$ _____

11. $(x+y)^4 \div (x+y)^7$ _____

12. $\frac{(c+d)^6}{(c+d)^9}$ _____

13. $d \div d^7$ _____

14. $\frac{(a+b)}{(a+b)^3}$ _____

15. $\frac{(y+3)^2}{(y+3)^{10}}$ _____

Roots and Powers

EXAMPLE   Evaluate the root $\sqrt[6]{x^6}$.

$\sqrt[6]{x^6} = x$, because $x \cdot x \cdot x \cdot x \cdot x \cdot x = x^6$

Directions Evaluate the roots. Explain your answer.

1. $\sqrt{25}$ _____

2. $\sqrt[3]{-27}$ _____

3. $\sqrt[4]{z^4}$ _____

4. $\sqrt{y^4}$ _____

5. $\sqrt[3]{-a^3}$ _____

6. $\sqrt[3]{x^{21}y^{33}}$ _____

EXAMPLE   Use the power rules to multiply exponents.

$(x^3)^4 = x^{(3)(4)} = x^{12}$

Remember, $(a^m)^n = a^{mn}$.

Directions Multiply. Use the power rules.

7. $(5^2)^2$ _____

8. $(2^5)^2$ _____

9. $(-x^3)^3$ _____

10. $(xy^5)^2$ _____

11. $(x^3y^4)^2$ _____

12. $(ab)^6$ _____

13. $(a^2b^2)^2$ _____

14. $(x^3y^4)^5$ _____

15. $(m^3n^3)^2$ _____

Operations with Radicals

EXAMPLES Find the sum of $\sqrt{a}$ and $2\sqrt{a}$. You may add radicals that are alike. $\sqrt{a} + 2\sqrt{a} = 3\sqrt{a}$

Find the difference of $3\sqrt{x}$ and $2\sqrt{x}$. You may subtract radicals that are alike.
$3\sqrt{x} - 2\sqrt{x} = \sqrt{x}$

Find the sum of $2\sqrt{y}$ and $3\sqrt{x}$. You cannot add or subtract unlike radicals.
$2\sqrt{y} + 3\sqrt{x} = 2\sqrt{y} + 3\sqrt{x}$

Directions Find the sums or differences.

1. $5\sqrt{2} + 6\sqrt{2}$ _____

2. $4\sqrt[3]{2} + 5\sqrt[3]{2}$ _____

3. $\sqrt[3]{x} + 3\sqrt{x}$ _____

4. $5\sqrt{2} - 4\sqrt{2}$ _____

5. $4\sqrt[3]{2} - 6\sqrt[3]{2}$ _____

6. $2\sqrt[3]{x} + 2\sqrt[3]{y}$ _____

7. $3\sqrt{(x + 1)} + 4\sqrt{(x + 1)}$ _____

8. $\sqrt[4]{x} + 2\sqrt[4]{x}$ _____

9. $3\sqrt{(y^2 + 1)} - 2\sqrt{(y^2 + 1)}$ _____

10. $\sqrt[5]{2} + \sqrt[6]{2}$ _____

EXAMPLES Simplify $12\sqrt{x^2 y}$.
$\sqrt{ab} = \sqrt{a}\sqrt{b}$, so $12\sqrt{x^2 y} = 12\sqrt{x^2}\sqrt{y} = 12x\sqrt{y}$.

Simplify $6\sqrt{\dfrac{x^4}{y}}$.
$\sqrt{\dfrac{a}{b}} = \dfrac{\sqrt{a}}{\sqrt{b}}$, so $6\sqrt{\dfrac{x^4}{y}} = 6\dfrac{\sqrt{x^4}}{\sqrt{y}} = \dfrac{6x^2}{\sqrt{y}}$

Directions Find the product or quotient. Give your answers in
simplified form.

11. $\sqrt{12}\sqrt{3}$ _____

12. $\sqrt{72}\sqrt{2}$ _____

13. $\sqrt{\dfrac{16}{25}}$ _____

14. $\sqrt{\dfrac{4a^2}{25b^2}}$ _____

15. $\sqrt[3]{-\dfrac{27}{64}}$ _____

16. $\sqrt{3}\sqrt{24}$ _____

17. $\dfrac{\sqrt[3]{-8}}{\sqrt[3]{27}}$ _____

18. $\sqrt[3]{\dfrac{16y^4}{2y}}$ _____

19. $(\sqrt[4]{x})(\sqrt[4]{x^3})$ _____

20. $(\sqrt[3]{(x^2 y^2)})(\sqrt[3]{xy})$ _____

Radical Equations

EXAMPLE   Solve for x: $8 = \sqrt{\dfrac{3}{x}}$

Square each side. $8^2 = (\sqrt{\dfrac{3}{x}})^2$

$64 = \dfrac{3}{x}$

Multiply each side by x. $64x = 3$

Divide each side by 64. $x = \dfrac{3}{64}$

Directions Find the unknown.

1. $\sqrt{x^2} + 5 = 30$ _____

2. $\sqrt{x} - 8 = 1$ _____

3. $3\sqrt{y} + 8 = 2\sqrt{y} - 4$ _____

4. $12 = \sqrt{\dfrac{2}{x}}$ _____

5. $4 = \dfrac{6}{\sqrt{y}}$ _____

6. $\sqrt[3]{x} + 1 = 5$ _____

7. $-6\sqrt{y} - 3 = 5 - 8\sqrt{y}$ _____

8. $\sqrt{\dfrac{x}{4}} = 8$ _____

9. $5 = \sqrt{x} + 1$ _____

10. $\sqrt{3 + y} = -8$ _____

11. $24 - \sqrt{x} = 27$ _____

12. $\sqrt{y - 6} = 8$ _____

13. $\sqrt{2x + 3} = \dfrac{5}{4}\sqrt{x + 5}$ _____

14. $\sqrt[3]{\dfrac{a}{8}} = 8$ _____

15. $\sqrt[3]{\dfrac{x}{2}} = 1$ _____

Fractional Exponential Notation

EXAMPLES   Rewrite, using fractional exponents.

$$\sqrt[3]{m} = m^{\frac{1}{3}}$$

$$\sqrt[3]{m^2} = m^{\frac{2}{3}}$$

$$\sqrt[3]{\sqrt{m}} = (m^{\frac{1}{2}})^{\frac{1}{3}} = m^{\frac{1}{6}}$$

Directions   Rewrite, using fractional exponents.

1. $\sqrt[3]{m^2}$ _____

2. $\sqrt{x}\sqrt{y^3}$ _____

3. $\sqrt[4]{x^3}$ _____

4. $\sqrt{a^3}\sqrt{b^3}$ _____

5. $\sqrt[3]{m}\sqrt{n}$ _____

6. $\sqrt[4]{x + y}$ _____

7. $\sqrt[4]{(x + y)^2}$ _____

8. $\sqrt[3]{\sqrt{x}}$ _____

9. $\sqrt[4]{\sqrt{a}}$ _____

10. $\dfrac{\sqrt[3]{m + n}}{\sqrt[3]{p + q}}$ _____

EXAMPLES   Find the product.

$$(a^{\frac{1}{2}})(a^{\frac{3}{2}}) = a^{\frac{1}{2} + \frac{3}{2}} = a^{\frac{4}{2}} = a^2$$

Find the quotient.

$$\frac{(a^{\frac{2}{3}})}{(a^{\frac{1}{3}})} = a^{\frac{2}{3} - \frac{1}{3}} = a^{\frac{1}{3}}$$

Directions   Find the products or quotients.

11. $(x^{\frac{1}{2}})(x^{\frac{1}{2}})$ _____

12. $(x^{\frac{1}{2}})(x^{\frac{2}{3}})$ _____

13. $(x^3)(x^{\frac{1}{2}})$ _____

14. $a^2 \div a^{\frac{1}{2}}$ _____

15. $x^{\frac{2}{3}} \div x^{\frac{1}{3}}$ _____

16. $x^{\frac{1}{2}} \div x^{\frac{2}{3}}$ _____

17. $x^{\frac{1}{2}} \div x^{\frac{1}{3}}$ _____

18. $x^{\frac{1}{3}} \div x^{\frac{1}{2}}$ _____

19. $(x^{-\frac{1}{2}})(x^{\frac{1}{2}})$ _____

20. $y^{\frac{5}{3}} \div y^2$ _____

Radicals in Fractions

EXAMPLE   Rewrite $\frac{5}{\sqrt{13}}$ so that its denominator is rational.

Multiply the numerator and denominator by the denominator.

$$\left(\frac{5}{\sqrt{13}}\right)\left(\frac{\sqrt{13}}{\sqrt{13}}\right) = \frac{5\sqrt{13}}{13}$$

Directions Rationalize the denominators.

1. $\dfrac{5}{\sqrt{2}}$ _____

2. $\dfrac{3}{\sqrt{3}}$ _____

3. $\dfrac{7}{\sqrt{a}}$ _____

4. $\dfrac{\sqrt{3}}{\sqrt{5}}$ _____

5. $\sqrt{\dfrac{a}{3}}$ _____

6. $\sqrt{\dfrac{4}{x}}$ _____

7. $\dfrac{5}{\sqrt{3x}}$ _____

8. $\dfrac{12}{\sqrt{3x}}$ _____

9. $\dfrac{6}{5\sqrt{2y}}$ _____

10. $\dfrac{6\sqrt{y}}{5\sqrt{2y}}$ _____

11. $\dfrac{3}{\sqrt{3-a}}$ _____

12. $\dfrac{5}{\sqrt{a-5}}$ _____

13. $\dfrac{x}{\sqrt{x+3}}$ _____

14. $\dfrac{2a}{\sqrt{a+2}}$ _____

15. $\dfrac{6y}{\sqrt{3y+7}}$ _____

Rationalizing with Conjugates

EXAMPLE   Rewrite $\dfrac{\sqrt{3}}{4\sqrt{3} - \sqrt{5}}$ so that its denominator is rational.

Multiply the numerator and denominator by the conjugate of the denominator, $4\sqrt{3} + \sqrt{5}$. The conjugate of $\sqrt{a} + \sqrt{b}$ is $\sqrt{a} - \sqrt{b}$; $(\sqrt{a} + \sqrt{b})(\sqrt{a} - \sqrt{b}) = a - b$.

$$\frac{\sqrt{3}}{4\sqrt{3} - \sqrt{5}}$$

$$= \frac{(\sqrt{3})(4\sqrt{3} + \sqrt{5})}{(4\sqrt{3} - \sqrt{5})(4\sqrt{3} + \sqrt{5})}$$

$$= \frac{(\sqrt{3})(4\sqrt{3} + \sqrt{5})}{(4\sqrt{3})^2 - (\sqrt{5})^2}$$

$$= \frac{(\sqrt{3})(4\sqrt{3} + \sqrt{5})}{(16)(3) - 5}$$

$$= \frac{(\sqrt{3})(4\sqrt{3} + \sqrt{5})}{48 - 5} = \frac{(\sqrt{3})(4\sqrt{3}) + \sqrt{3}\sqrt{5}}{43} = \frac{12 + \sqrt{15}}{43}$$

Directions   Rationalize the denominators.

1. $\dfrac{5}{\sqrt{3} - \sqrt{5}}$ _____

2. $\dfrac{3}{2\sqrt{5} + \sqrt{7}}$ _____

3. $\dfrac{7}{\sqrt{7} - \sqrt{5}}$ _____

4. $\dfrac{9}{\sqrt{3} + \sqrt{2}}$ _____

5. $\dfrac{a}{\sqrt{a} + \sqrt{2}}$ _____

6. $\dfrac{3}{2\sqrt{a} - \sqrt{3}}$ _____

7. $\dfrac{a}{3\sqrt{7} - \sqrt{5}}$ _____

8. $\dfrac{3}{2\sqrt{5} + \sqrt{13}}$ _____

9. $\dfrac{x}{2\sqrt{x} + \sqrt{3}}$ _____

10. $\dfrac{2a}{2\sqrt{a} + 3\sqrt{a}}$ _____

Rational Numbers and Decimals

EXAMPLES

Write $\frac{2}{3}$ as a decimal.

$\frac{2}{3} = 2 \div 3$ or $3\overline{)2.0\,0\,0\,0}$
$$\begin{array}{r} 0.6\,6\,6... \\ \hline \end{array}$$

$$\begin{array}{r} 1\,8 \\ \hline 2\,0 \\ 1\,8 \\ \hline 2\,0 \end{array}$$

$\frac{2}{3} = 0.666 \ldots$ may be written as $0.\overline{6}$.

Write $\frac{1}{2}$ as a decimal.

$\frac{1}{2} = 1 \div 2$ or $2\overline{)1.0\,0}$
$$\begin{array}{r} 0.5\,0 \\ \hline \end{array}$$

$$\begin{array}{r} 1\,0 \\ \hline 0 \end{array}$$

$\frac{1}{2} = 0.5\overline{0}$, where $\overline{0}$ means that the zero is repeated infinitely many times.

Directions Write as decimals. Use bar notation for repeating digits.

1. $\frac{3}{4}$ _____

2. $\frac{1}{5}$ _____

3. $\frac{1}{6}$ _____

4. $\frac{1}{7}$ _____

5. $\frac{1}{8}$ _____

6. $\frac{1}{9}$ _____

7. $1\frac{2}{5}$ _____

8. $1\frac{5}{6}$ _____

9. $2\frac{2}{7}$ _____

10. $3\frac{3}{8}$ _____

11. $\frac{1}{16}$ _____

12. $\frac{1}{32}$ _____

13. $\frac{1}{11}$ _____

14. $\frac{2}{9}$ _____

15. $2\frac{3}{32}$ _____

Decimal Expansions and Rational Numbers

EXAMPLE Write $0.\overline{7}$ as a rational number.

Let x = rational number.

$x = 0.\overline{7}$ Multiply by 10 to place the repeating part of the decimal to the left of the decimal point.

$10x = 7.\overline{7}$ Subtract $x = 0.\overline{7}$ to subtract repeating digits.

$-x = -0.\overline{7}$ $(0.\overline{7} - 0.\overline{7} = 0)$

$9x = 7.0$

$x = \frac{7}{9}$

Directions Write as rational numbers.

1. $0.\overline{5}$ _____

2. $0.\overline{100}$ _____

3. $1.\overline{01}$ _____

4. $0.\overline{571428}$ _____

5. $0.\overline{8}$ _____

6. $0.\overline{63}$ _____

7. $0.\overline{36}$ _____

8. $0.\overline{300}$ _____

9. $2.\overline{36}$ _____

10. $1.\overline{84}$ _____

Geometry Connection: Radicals and Triangles

EXAMPLE   Find the unknown length to the nearest hundredth.

$z^2 = x^2 + y^2$ Substitute values for x and y, then solve.
$z^2 = 6^2 + 12^2$
$z = \sqrt{36 + 144} = \sqrt{180}$
A calculator gives $\sqrt{180}$ as 13.416407 . . .
Rounding to the nearest hundredth gives 13.42.
$z \approx 13.42$

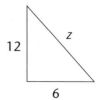

Directions Find the unknown length to the nearest hundredth.
Use your calculator.

1. $x = 7, y = 8$ _____

2. $x = 9, y = 11$ _____

3. $x = 5, y = 3$ _____

4. $x = 3, y = 7$ _____

5. $x = 12, y = 14$ _____

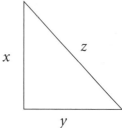

EXAMPLE   Find the unknown length to the nearest thousandth.

Substitute known values in $z^2 = x^2 + y^2$ and
solve for the unknown.
$9^2 = x^2 + 4^2$
$x^2 = 9^2 - 4^2$
$x = \sqrt{81 - 16} = \sqrt{65}$
A calculator gives $\sqrt{65}$ as 8.06225 . . .
Rounding to the nearest thousandth gives 8.062.
$x \approx 8.062$

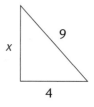

Directions Find the unknown length to the nearest thousandth.
Use your calculator.

6. $x = 4, z = 11$ _____

7. $y = 3, z = 6$ _____

8. $x = 16, z = 44$ _____

9. $x = 8, z = 11$ _____

10. $y = 5, z = 9$ _____

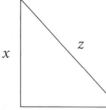

Exponential Functions

EXAMPLE   Let $f(x) = 5^x$. Evaluate the function for $x = 2, 0,$ and -3.

x	$f(x) = 5^x$	$f(x)$
2	$f(2) = 5^2$	25
0	$f(0) = 5^0$	1
-3	$f(-3) = 5^{-3}$	$\frac{1}{125}$

Directions   Evaluate the function $f(x) = 2^x$ for the values of x given.

1. $x = 0$ _____

2. $x = 1$ _____

3. $x = 2$ _____

4. $x = 3$ _____

5. $x = 4$ _____

6. $x = 6$ _____

7. $x = 7$ _____

8. $x = -1$ _____

9. $x = -3$ _____

10. $x = -5$ _____

11. $x = 10$ _____

12. $x = -10$ _____

Directions   Evaluate the function $f(x) = \left(\frac{1}{2}\right)^x$ for the values of x given.

13. $x = 0$ _____

14. $x = 1$ _____

15. $x = 2$ _____

16. $x = 3$ _____

17. $x = 4$ _____

18. $x = -1$ _____

19. $x = -2$ _____

20. $x = -3$ _____

21. $x = -4$ _____

22. $x = -5$ _____

23. $x = 10$ _____

24. $x = -10$ _____

Directions   Draw the graph of the points in problems 1–6. Connect the points with a smooth curve.

25.

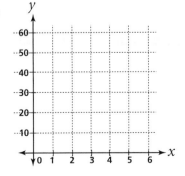

Exponents of Base 10

EXAMPLE   Use the table below to solve for x. $10^x = 4$.

10^0	1
$10^{0.301}$	≈ 2
$10^{0.477}$	≈ 3
$10^{0.699}$	≈ 5
$10^{0.778}$	≈ 6
$10^{0.845}$	≈ 7
10^1	10

$4 = (2)(2)$ and $2 \approx 10^{0.301}$
So $10^x = (2)(2) \approx (10^{0.301})(10^{0.301}) = 10^{(0.301 + 0.301)} = 10^{0.602}$.
Therefore, $10^x \approx 10^{0.602}$ and $x \approx 0.602$.

Directions   Use the values from the table above to calculate the values of x.

1. $10^x = 9$ _____   **9.** $10^x = 35$ _____

2. $10^x = 12$ _____   **10.** $10^x = 50$ _____

3. $10^x = 14$ _____   **11.** $10^x = 60$ _____

4. $10^x = 15$ _____   **12.** $10^x = 100$ _____

5. $10^x = 18$ _____   **13.** $10^x = 140$ _____

6. $10^x = 20$ _____   **14.** $10^x = 150$ _____

7. $10^x = 21$ _____   **15.** $10^x = 210$ _____

8. $10^x = 30$ _____   **16.** $10^x = 350$ _____

Directions   Estimate, using the values given above, to determine if the statements below seem reasonable. Write *yes* or *no*.

17. $10^{0.399} \approx 4$ _____

18. $10^{1.992} \approx 11$ _____

19. $10^{0.9555} \approx 9$ _____

20. $10^{1.8} \approx 20$ _____

Scientific Notation: Using Powers of 10

EXAMPLE   Write 0.000843 in scientific notation.

$0.0008 43 = 8.43 \times 10^{-4}$
The decimal point moves four spaces to the right.

Directions Write the values below in scientific notation.

1. 83,490 _____

2. 0.005783 _____

3. 10,000,000 _____

4. 54,932 _____

5. 0.0000783 _____

6. 284.3972 _____

7. 900.3721×10^5 _____

8. 0.8326183×10^4 _____

9. 754.32×10^{-6} _____

10. $16,000,000 \times 10^{-2}$ _____

EXAMPLE   Write 1.5983785×10^{10} in standard form.

$1.5983785000 \times 10^{10} = 15,983,785,000$
The decimal point moves 10 spaces to the right.

Directions Write the values below in standard form.

11. 8.4×10^4 _____

12. 7.49×10^9 _____

13. 9.03×10^{-3} _____

14. 7.036×10^{-2} _____

15. 1.02045×10^7 _____

16. 4.52×10^6 _____

17. 1.1×10^{-8} _____

18. 9.20450912×10^2 _____

19. 5×10^{-4} _____

20. 3.724×10^8 _____

Exponential Equations

<table>
<tr><td>**EXAMPLE**</td><td>Solve for x: $4^{(x + 1)} = 4^{(3x - 5)}$

The bases are equal, so the exponents are equal.

$x + 1 = 3x - 5$

$x - 3x = -5 - 1$

$-2x = -6$

$x = 3$</td></tr>
</table>

Directions Solve for x.

1. $8^x = 8^{(2x + 4)}$ _____

2. $2^{3x} = 2^{(2x + 1)}$ _____

3. $4^{(x - 3)} = 4^{(4x + 4)}$ _____

4. $5^{(x + 3)} = 5^{(5x - 1)}$ _____

5. $10^x = 10^{(3x + 7)}$ _____

6. $m^{(2x + 2)} = m^{(4x - 3)}$ _____

7. $a^x = a^{2x}$ _____

8. $5^{(4x + 1)} = 25^x$ _____

9. $10^x = 1{,}000^{(x + 1)}$ _____

10. $a^{6x} = a^{(3x + 2)}$ _____

<table>
<tr><td>**EXAMPLE**</td><td>Solve for x: $\sqrt{4^{(x + 1)}} = \sqrt{2^{(x + 1)}}$

$4^{\frac{(x + 1)}{2}} = 2^{\frac{(x + 1)}{2}}$

$2^{\frac{2(x + 1)}{2}} = 2^{\frac{(x + 1)}{2}}$

$2^{(x + 1)} = 2^{\frac{(x + 1)}{2}}$

$x + 1 = \frac{(x + 1)}{2}$

$2x + 2 = x + 1$

$x = -1$</td></tr>
</table>

Directions Solve for x.

11. $\sqrt{3^{(x + 2)}} = \sqrt{9^{2x}}$ _____

12. $\sqrt{5^{4x}} = \sqrt{25^{(x + 4)}}$ _____

13. $\sqrt{a^x} = \sqrt{a^{(2x - 3)}}$ _____

14. $\sqrt{a^{4x}} = \sqrt{a^{(3x + 2)}}$ _____

15. $\sqrt[3]{a^{(6x + 3)}} = \sqrt{a^{2x}}$ _____

The Number *e*, Base *e*

EXAMPLE   Use your calculator to evaluate $f(x) = e^x$ for $x = 2$.
Press [2nd] [LN] 2 [ENTER]. The display reads *7.389056099*.
So, $f(2) = e^2 \approx 7.389$.

Directions Use your calculator to evaluate $f(x) = e^x$ for the given values.
Write your answers in scientific notation.

	x	e^x	
1.	$x = 0$	$e^0 = ?$	
2.	$x = 1$	$e^1 = ?$	
3.	$x = 2$	$e^2 = ?$	
4.	$x = 5$	$e^5 = ?$	
5.	$x = 10$	$e^{10} = ?$	
6.	$x = 50$	$e^{50} = ?$	
7.	$x = 60$	$e^{60} = ?$	
8.	$x = 100$	$e^{100} = ?$	
9.	$x = 150$	$e^{150} = ?$	
10.	$x = 200$	$e^{200} = ?$	

Directions Use your calculator to evaluate $f(x) = e^{-x}$ for the given
values. Write your answers in scientific notation.

	x	e^{-x}	
11.	$x = 0$	$e^0 = ?$	
12.	$x = 3$	$e^{-3} = ?$	
13.	$x = 4$	$e^{-4} = ?$	
14.	$x = 15$	$e^{-15} = ?$	
15.	$x = 20$	$e^{-20} = ?$	
16.	$x = 30$	$e^{-30} = ?$	
17.	$x = 40$	$e^{-40} = ?$	
18.	$x = 60$	$e^{-60} = ?$	
19.	$x = 120$	$e^{-120} = ?$	
20.	$x = 140$	$e^{-140} = ?$	

Inverse Functions

EXAMPLE   Given the function of f: (3, 4) (−2, 0) (4, −2) (−1, −3)

f^{-1}: (4, 3) (0, −2) (−2, 4) (−3, −1)

Directions For each set of ordered pairs, write the inverse.

1. f: (2, 1) (3, −1) (0, 5)   _____

2. f: (−1, −1) (2, 2) (4, 4) (−3, −3)   _____

3. f: (17, 3) (−22, −8) (10, −10) (14, −24)   _____

4. f: (a, b) (c, d) (e, g) (m, n) _____

EXAMPLE   Find the equation for f^{-1} if $f(x) = 3x - 2$.

$f(x) = y = 3x - 2$
$x = 3y - 2$
$x + 2 = 3y$
$\frac{x + 2}{3} = y$
$y = \frac{x}{3} + \frac{2}{3}$
$f^{-1}(x) = \frac{x}{3} + \frac{2}{3}$

Directions Find the equation for $f^{-1}(x)$.

5. $f(x) = -2x$ _____

6. $f(x) = x + 4$ _____

7. $f(x) = 5x - 10$ _____

8. $f(x) = -3x + 12$ _____

9. $f(x) = 8x + 4$ _____

10. $f(x) = \frac{1}{2}x - 4$ _____

11. $f(x) = -\frac{2}{3}x - 6$ _____

12. $f(x) = 3x - 7$ _____

13. $f(x) = -6x + 3$ _____

14. $f(x) = \sqrt{x - 3}$ _____

15. $f(x) = \sqrt{4x + 1}$ _____

Translation of Exponents and Logarithms

(**EXAMPLE**)   Write $2^7 = 128$ in logarithmic form.
$\log_2 128 = 7$

Directions Write the equations in logarithmic form.

1. $3^6 = 729$ _____

2. $2^4 = 16$ _____

3. $7^3 = 343$ _____

4. $10^3 = 1,000$ _____

5. $9^4 = 6,561$ _____

6. $e^3 \approx 20.086$ _____

7. $e^{10} \approx 22,026.466$ _____

8. $8^x = 64$ _____

9. $e^x = 403.429$ _____

10. $m^x = n$ _____

(**EXAMPLE**)   Write $\log_5 25 = 2$ in exponential form.
$5^2 = 25$

Directions Write the equations in exponential form.

11. $\log_3 9 = 2$ _____

12. $\log_5 625 = 4$ _____

13. $\log_8 32,768 = 5$ _____

14. $\log_{10} 10,000 = 4$ _____

15. $\log_{16} 256 = 2$ _____

16. $\ln 148.413 = 5$ _____

17. $\ln 54.6 = 2x$ _____

18. $\log_x 120 = 2.5$ _____

19. $\ln y = x$ _____

20. $\log_a b = x$ _____

Logarithmic Functions and Their Properties

$\boxed{\text{EXAMPLE}}$ Express $\log_3(9)(27)$ as a sum.

$\log_3(9)(27) = \log_3 9 + \log_3 27$

Directions Express as a sum of logarithms.

1. $\log_b MN$ _____

2. $\log_{10}(10)(100)$ _____

3. $\ln(5)(8)$ _____

4. $\log_5 AB$ _____

5. $\ln(xy)$ _____

6. $\log_4 15$ _____

7. $\log_x 10$ _____

8. $\ln 7^2$ _____

9. $\log_{10} x^2$ _____

10. $\log_x(ab)$ _____

$\boxed{\text{EXAMPLE}}$ Express $\log_2(\frac{9}{4})$ as a difference.

$\log_2(\frac{9}{4}) = \log_2 9 - \log_2 4$

Directions Express as a difference of logarithms.

11. $\ln(\frac{10}{3})$ _____

12. $\log_2(\frac{20}{3})$ _____

13. $\log_x(\frac{2}{3})$ _____

14. $\ln(\frac{x}{y})$ _____

15. $\log_{10}(\frac{3x}{y})$ _____

16. $\log_x \frac{(a+b)}{c}$ _____

$\boxed{\text{EXAMPLE}}$ Rewrite the expression $\log_3 8^{-4}$ as a product.

$\log_3 8^{-4} = -4\log_3 8$

Directions Express as a product of the exponent and the logarithm.

17. $\log_{10} 5^4$ _____

18. $\ln 8^x$ _____

19. $\log_3 \sqrt[3]{18}$ _____

20. $\ln \sqrt[y]{x}$ _____

Logarithmic Equations

EXAMPLES   Solve for x. $4^x = 14$

$$\log_{10}4^x = \log_{10}14$$
$$x\log_{10}4 = \log_{10}14$$
$$x = \frac{\log_{10}14}{\log_{10}4}$$
$$x \approx \frac{1.146}{0.602}$$
$$x \approx 1.904$$

Solve for x. $3^{(2x + 2)} = 15$

$$\log_{10}3^{(2x + 2)} = \log_{10}15$$
$$(2x + 4)\log_{10}3 = \log_{10}15$$
$$2x + 4 = \frac{\log_{10}15}{\log_{10}3}$$
$$2x = \left(\frac{\log_{10}15}{\log_{10}3}\right) - 4$$
$$x = \frac{\left(\frac{\log_{10}15}{\log_{10}3}\right) - 4}{2}$$
$$x \approx \frac{\left(\frac{1.176}{0.477} - 4\right)}{2}$$
$$x \approx \frac{(2.465 - 4)}{2}$$
$$x \approx \frac{-1.535}{2}$$
$$x \approx -0.768$$

Directions Rewrite as a logarithmic equation. Then solve for x. Use your calculator. Round decimals to the nearest thousandth.

1. $5^x = 30$ _____

2. $2^x = 10$ _____

3. $6^x = 600$ _____

4. $5^x = 100$ _____

5. $7^x = 8$ _____

6. $10^x = 12,800$ _____

7. $3^x = 1,750$ _____

8. $15 + 9^x = 100$ _____

9. $16 - 2^x = 8$ _____

10. $4^{(2x + 1)} = 20$ _____

11. $2^{(x - 5)} = 12$ _____

12. $10^{3x} = 450$ _____

13. $15^{(5x + 3)} = 90$ _____

Directions Solve each problem.

14. A study of the population growth in a certain city determined that the growth in population P is represented by the formula $P = 120,000(10^{0.021t})$. In this formula, $t =$ time in years and 120,000 is the population of the city when it was first studied. How long will it take, to the nearest half-year, for the city to double its population? _____

15. A bacterial culture is growing according to the formula $y = 50,000e^{0.8x}$. In this formula, x is the time in days and y is the number of bacteria. Estimate the number of bacteria after 1 month. (Hint: Assume there are 30 days in the month.) _____

Geometry Connection: π

EXAMPLE   Calculate the volume of a sphere with a radius of 10 yards.
Estimate to the nearest thousandth.

$V = \frac{4}{3}\pi r^3$ $r = 10$ yards

$V = \frac{4}{3}\pi (10)^3$

$V = \frac{4}{3}\pi \, 1{,}000$

$V = \frac{4{,}000\pi}{3}$ cubic yards

$V \approx 4{,}188.790$ cubic yards

Directions Calculate the volume of each object. Leave π in your answer.
Then, using a calculator, calculate the answer to the
nearest thousandth.

1. A sphere with a radius of 10 in.   _____

2. A cone with a radius of 4 in. and a height of 20 in.   _____

3. A cylinder with a height of 2 m and a radius of 5 m   _____

4. A sphere with a diameter of 6 ft   _____

5. A cylinder with a height of 10 ft and a diameter of 20 ft   _____

6. A cone with a diameter of 18 m and a height of 10 m   _____

EXAMPLE   Solve the formula for r: $d = rt$.

$\frac{d}{t} = \frac{rt}{t}$

$r = \frac{d}{t}$

Directions Solve the formula for the variable indicated.

7. $A = \frac{\pi dl}{2}$; solve for l.   _____

8. $A = \frac{\pi dl}{2}$; solve for d.   _____

9. $V = (\frac{1}{3})\pi r^2 h$; solve for r.   _____

10. $V = \pi r^2 h$; solve for h.   _____

Introduction—The Circle

EXAMPLE   Write the equation of a circle with its center at $(-2, 4)$ and a radius of $\sqrt{6}$.

The standard form for a circle whose center is at (h, k) is $(x - h)^2 + (y - k)^2 = r^2$.
Substitute $h = -2$, $k = 4$, and $r = \sqrt{6}$.

$$[x - (-2)]^2 + (y - 4)^2 = (\sqrt{6})^2$$
$$(x + 2)^2 + (y - 4)^2 = 6$$

Directions Write the equation of the circle with the given center and
radius.

1. $(6, 4), r = 8$ _____

2. $(-4, 3), r = 5$ _____

3. $(-3, 3), r = 7$ _____

4. $(5, 7), r = \sqrt{7}$ _____

5. $(-4, -8), r = 9$ _____

EXAMPLE   What is the center and the radius of a circle whose equation is
$(x - 6)^2 + (y + 4)^2 = 121$?
Compare to standard form: $(x - h)^2 + (y - k)^2 = r^2$

$x - h = x - 6$	$y - k = y + 4$	$r^2 = 81$
$h = 6$	$k = -4$	$r = \sqrt{81} = 9$

Center is at $(6, -4)$; radius $= 9$

Directions Give the center and radius of each circle.

6. $(x + 2)^2 + (y - 3)^2 = 9$ _____

7. $(x - 4)^2 + (y + 9)^2 = 10$ _____

8. $(x + 5)^2 + (y - 5)^2 = 64$ _____

9. $(x - 8)^2 + (y + 12)^2 = 169$ _____

10. $(x + \frac{1}{2})^2 + (y - \frac{1}{3})^2 = \frac{16}{25}$ _____

Completing the Square: Circles

EXAMPLE Find the center and radius, then sketch the circle: $(x - 4)^2 + (y + 3)^2 = 25$.

Compare the equation for the circle to the standard form
for a circle whose center is at (h, k): $(x - h)^2 + (y - k)^2 = r^2$.

Find the circle's center and radius.

$x - h = x - 4$ $y - k = y + 3$ $r^2 = 25$
$\quad\quad h = 4$ $\quad\quad k = -3$ $\quad\quad r = \sqrt{25} = 5$

Center is at $(4, -3)$; radius = 5

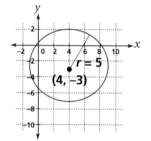

Directions Find the center and radius of each circle.
Then sketch the circle on graph paper.

1. $x^2 + y^2 = 9$ _____

2. $(x + 2)^2 + (y - 1)^2 = 4$ _____

3. $(x - 3)^2 + (y + 2)^2 = 9$ _____

EXAMPLE Change $x^2 + y^2 + 6x - 8y + 9 = 0$ to standard form. Then find the center and radius.

Step 1 Group all the x- and y-terms on the left and move constants
to the right side of the equation. $(x^2 + 6x +$ ___$) + (y^2 - 8y +$ ___$) = -9$

Step 2 Complete the square for the x- and y-terms.

$(x^2 + 6x + [(\frac{1}{2})6]^2)$ $(y^2 - 8y + [(\frac{1}{2})(-8)]^2)$

$(x^2 + 6x + 9)$ $+$ $(y^2 - 8y + 16) = -9 + 9 + 16$

Add the squared terms to both sides of the equation.

Step 3 Factor to place in standard form: $(x + 3)^2 + (y - 4)^2 = 16$

Step 4 Determine the circle's center and radius.

$x - h = x + 3$ $y - k = y - 4$ $r^2 = 16$
$\quad\quad h = -3$ $\quad\quad k = 4$ $\quad\quad r = \sqrt{16} = 4$

Center is at $(-3, 4)$; radius = 4

Directions Change to standard form by completing the square.
Give the center and the radius.

4. $x^2 + y^2 - 8y = 0$ _____

5. $x^2 + y^2 + 10x - 16y + 11 = 0$ _____

Ellipses

EXAMPLE Write $x^2 + 4y^2 = 16$ in standard form for an ellipse with its center at (0, 0).

Compare the equation to standard form: $\frac{x^2}{a^2} + \frac{y^2}{b^2} = 1$

$x^2 + 4y^2 = 16$

Divide each side by 16. $\frac{x^2}{16} + \frac{y^2}{4} = 1$

Directions Rewrite in standard form for an ellipse with its center
at $(0, 0)$.

1. $9x^2 + y^2 = 9$ _____

2. $x^2 + 25y^2 = 25$ _____

3. $16x^2 + y^2 = 16$ _____

4. $3x^2 + y^2 = 27$ _____

5. $4x^2 + 2y^2 = 8$ _____

6. $2x^2 + 8y^2 = 32$ _____

EXAMPLE Sketch the ellipse $\frac{x^2}{25} + \frac{y^2}{16} = 1$.

Step 1 Find vertices—the x- and y-intercepts. Compare the equation to the standard
form for an ellipse with its center at (0, 0): $\frac{x^2}{a^2} + \frac{y^2}{b^2} = 1$.

Let $y = 0$ $a^2 = 25$, $a = \pm 5$, x-intercepts
Let $x = 0$ $b^2 = 16$, $b = \pm 4$, y-intercepts

Step 2 The center is at (0, 0). Therefore, the major and
minor axes lie along the x- and y-axes. Because $a > b$,
the major axis and foci are along the x-axis
and $a^2 = b^2 + c^2$.
$25 = 16 + c^2$
$9 = c^2$, $c = \pm 3$; the foci are at (3, 0) and (−3, 0).

Step 3 Sketch the ellipse by plotting the x- and y-intercepts:
(5, 0), (−5, 0), (0, 4), (0, −4). Plot the center (0, 0).
Draw a smooth curve connecting the x- and y-intercepts.

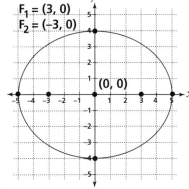

Directions Give the vertices and foci of each ellipse.
Then sketch the curve on graph paper.

7. $\frac{x^2}{16} + \frac{y^2}{25} = 1$ _____

8. $\frac{x^2}{100} + \frac{y^2}{36} = 1$ _____

9. $\frac{x^2}{9} + \frac{y^2}{4} = 1$ _____

10. $\frac{x^2}{49} + \frac{y^2}{81} = 1$ _____

Completing the Square: Ellipses

EXAMPLE   Find the center, vertices, and foci of the ellipse $\frac{(x-1)^2}{4} + \frac{(y-2)^2}{1} = 1$. Then sketch the ellipse.

Step 1 Find the center of the ellipse. Compare the equation to the standard form for an ellipse with its center at (h, k):

$\frac{(x-h)^2}{a^2} + \frac{(y-k)^2}{b^2} = 1$.

$x - h = x - 1$ $y - k = y - 2$
$\qquad h = 1$ $k = 2$ The center is at $(1, 2)$.

Find a and b.
Let $y = 0$ $a^2 = 4$, $a = \pm 2$
Let $x = 0$ $b^2 = 1$, $b = \pm 1$

Step 2 Determine the vertices. $a > b \rightarrow$ the major axis is parallel to the x-axis, along line $y = 2$.
Vertices along the major axis are ([center $\pm$ a], 2) =
([1 + a], 2) $\rightarrow$ ([1 + 2], 2) $\rightarrow$ (3, 2) and
([1 − a], 2) $\rightarrow$ ([1 − 2], 2) $\rightarrow$ (−1, 2).
Vertices along the minor axis are (1, [center $\pm$ b]) =
(1, [2 + b]) $\rightarrow$ (1, [2 + 1]) $\rightarrow$ (1, 3) and
(1, [2 − b]) $\rightarrow$ (1, [2 − 1]) $\rightarrow$ (1, 1).

Step 3 Determine the foci. $a > b \rightarrow$ and $a^2 = b^2 + c^2$
$4 = 1 + c^2$
$3 = c^2$, $c = \pm\sqrt{3}$
c is the distance along the major axis
from the center of the ellipse to a focus, so
$F_1 = ([1 + \sqrt{3}], 2)$ and $F_2 = ([1 - \sqrt{3}], 2)$.

Step 4 Sketch the ellipse. First, plot the center, (1, 2), of the ellipse. Next, plot the vertices. Connect the vertices with a smooth curve.

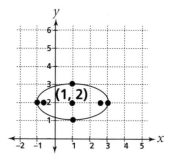

Directions   Find the center, vertices, and foci of each ellipse. Then sketch the curve on graph paper.

1. $\frac{(x+1)^2}{49} + \frac{(y-2)^2}{36} = 1$ _____

2. $\frac{(x+3)^2}{36} + \frac{(y-4)^2}{100} = 1$ _____

3. $\frac{(x+2)^2}{25} + \frac{(y+4)^2}{4} = 1$ _____

4. $\frac{(x-1)^2}{100} + \frac{(y+1)^2}{64} = 1$ _____

5. $\frac{(x-3)^2}{36} + \frac{(y+2)^2}{25} = 1$ _____

Hyperbolas

EXAMPLE

Write the equations of the asymptotes for the hyperbola

$\frac{x^2}{64} - \frac{y^2}{36} = 1$. Tell which axis contains the foci.

Compare the equation to the standard form for a hyperbola with its

center at $(0, 0)$: $\frac{x^2}{a^2} - \frac{y^2}{b^2} = 1 \rightarrow a^2 = 64$, $a = \pm8$; $b^2 = 36$, $b = \pm6$

Foci are on the x-axis for $\frac{x^2}{a^2} - \frac{y^2}{b^2} = 1$, so

the foci for $\frac{x^2}{64} - \frac{y^2}{36} = 1$ are on the x-axis.

Asymptotes are $y = \frac{b}{a}x$ and $y = -\frac{b}{a}x$, so

$y = \frac{b}{a}x = \frac{3}{4}x$ and $y = -\frac{b}{a}x = -\frac{3}{4}x$.

Directions Write the equations of the asymptotes for each hyperbola.
Then tell which axis contains the foci. Write *x-axis* or *y-axis*.

1. $\frac{x^2}{25} - \frac{y^2}{9} = 1$ _____

2. $\frac{y^2}{36} - \frac{x^2}{25} = 1$ _____

3. $\frac{y^2}{169} - \frac{x^2}{144} = 1$ _____

4. $\frac{x^2}{49} - \frac{y^2}{16} = 1$ _____

5. $\frac{x^2}{9} - \frac{y^2}{4} = 1$ _____

6. $\frac{y^2}{36} - \frac{x^2}{4} = 1$ _____

EXAMPLE

Sketch the hyperbola $\frac{x^2}{16} - \frac{y^2}{9} = 1$. Find the center, vertices, asymptotes, and foci.

Step 1 Find the center and vertices. Compare to the standard

form for a hyperbola with its center at $(0, 0)$: $\frac{x^2}{a^2} - \frac{y^2}{b^2} = 1$.

The center is at $(0, 0)$. To find the vertices, solve for a and b.
$a^2 = 16$, $a = \pm4$; $b^2 = 9$, $b = \pm3$

When $x = 0$, y is imaginary, therefore the vertices are the
x-intercepts $\pm a = \pm4$, or $(4, 0)$ and $(-4, 0)$.

Step 2 Determine the asymptotes: $y = \frac{b}{a}x \rightarrow y = \frac{3}{4}x$ and

$y = -\frac{b}{a}x \rightarrow y = -\frac{3}{4}x$

Step 3 Find c, the distance from the center to the foci.
$c^2 = a^2 + b^2$
$c^2 = 16 + 9 = 25$
$c = \pm\sqrt{25} = \pm5$, so foci are at ±5 along the x-axis:
$F_1 = (5, 0)$ and $F_2 = (-5, 0)$.

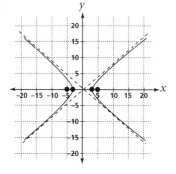

Step 4 Graph the vertices, asymptotes, and foci, then sketch the hyperbola.

Directions Sketch the hyperbolas. Find the center, vertices, asymptotes, and foci.

7. $\frac{x^2}{64} - \frac{y^2}{36} = 1$ **8.** $\frac{y^2}{64} - \frac{x^2}{49} = 1$ **9.** $\frac{x^2}{100} - \frac{y^2}{36} = 1$ **10.** $\frac{y^2}{9} - \frac{x^2}{16} = 1$

Completing the Square: Hyperbolas

EXAMPLE Given the hyperbola $\frac{(x-2)^2}{9} - \frac{(y+3)^2}{1} = 1$, find the center, asymptotes, vertices, and foci. Then sketch the curve.

Step 1 Compare to the standard form: $\frac{(x-h)^2}{a^2} - \frac{(y-k)^2}{b^2} = 1$.

Solve for the hyperbola's center.

$x - h = x - 2 \quad y - k = y + 3$
$\qquad h = 2 \qquad\qquad k = -3 \quad$ Center is at $(2, -3)$.

Step 2 Determine the asymptotes: $y = \frac{b}{a}x$ and $y = -\frac{b}{a}x$.

$a^2 = 9, a = \pm 3; b^2 = 1, b = \pm 1$

$y = \frac{b}{a}x \rightarrow y = \frac{1}{3}x; y = -\frac{b}{a}x \rightarrow y = -\frac{1}{3}x$

Asymptotes pass through the hyperbola's center, $(2, -3)$.

Step 3 Vertices are on the line $y = -3$ at
$([\text{center} \pm a], -3)$: $([2 + 3], -3)$ and $([2 - 3], -3)$.
Vertices are $(5, -3)$ and $(-1, -3)$.

Step 4 Foci are on the line $y = -3$ at a distance of $\pm c$
from the center, $(2, -3)$. $F = ([2 \pm c], -3)$.
$c^2 = a^2 + b^2 = 9 + 1 = 10; c = \pm\sqrt{10}$
So $F_1 = ([2 + \sqrt{10}], -3)$ and $F_2 = ([2 - \sqrt{10}], -3)$.

Step 5 Sketch the curve. Plot the center first, then the
asymptotes. When drawing asymptotes, use
the hyperbola's center, $(2, -3)$, as if it were the origin.
Next, mark vertices and foci.

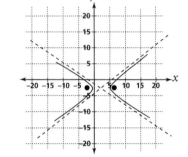

Directions Find the center, asymptotes, vertices, and foci for each hyperbola.

1. $\frac{(y-1)^2}{9} - \frac{(x+3)^2}{4} = 1$ _____

2. $\frac{(y-3)^2}{64} - \frac{(x+2)^2}{36} = 1$ _____

3. $\frac{(x-2)^2}{9} - \frac{(y-5)^2}{1} = 1$ _____

4. $\frac{(x+4)^2}{16} - \frac{(y+1)^2}{36} = 1$ _____

5. $\frac{(x+2)^2}{49} - \frac{(y-3)^2}{16} = 1$ _____

Parabolas

Given the parabola $y^2 = 16x$, find the vertex, focus, and directrix.

Compare to standard forms: $x^2 = 4py$ or $y^2 = 4px$.

$y^2 = 16x$ matches the standard form $y^2 = 4px$.
According to the definition, the vertex $= (0, 0)$.

$y^2 = 16x$, and $y^2 = 4px$, so $16x = 4px$ and $p = 4$.

By definition, the focus $= (p, 0)$. Substituting gives $(4, 0)$.

By definition, the directrix is $x = -p$. Substituting gives $x = -4$.

Sketch the graph, using the vertex, focus, and
directrix as guides. This is not a function;
there is more than one y-value for a single x-value.

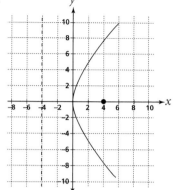

Directions Find the vertex, focus, and directrix for each parabola.
Sketch the curve and tell whether the parabola is a function
or not a function.

1. $x^2 = 24y$ _____

2. $x^2 = 8y$ _____

3. $x^2 = -\frac{1}{2}y$ _____

4. $y^2 = 8x$ _____

5. $y^2 = -\frac{1}{4}x$ _____

6. $y^2 = -2x$ _____

Write the equation of a parabola with focus $(0, 20)$ and directrix $y = -20$.

Because the focus $(0, 20)$ is on the y-axis, the standard form $4py = x^2$
applies and $(0, p)$ is defined as the focus. $(0, p) = (0, 20) \rightarrow p = 20$.

Substitute for p in $4py = x^2$; $4(20)y = x^2$, or $80y = x^2$.

Directions Write the equation of each parabola.

7. Focus $(10, 0)$; directrix $x = -10$ _____

8. Focus $\left(-\frac{3}{8}, 0\right)$; directrix $x = \frac{3}{8}$ _____

9. Focus $(0, -4)$; directrix $y = 4$ _____

10. Focus $\left(\frac{1}{4}, 0\right)$; directrix $x = -\frac{1}{4}$ _____

Completing the Square: Parabolas

EXAMPLE Given $(y - 1)^2 = -\frac{7}{8}(x - 6)$, find the vertex, focus, and directrix for the parabola. Describe the axis of symmetry.

Compare to the standard forms:
$(x - h)^2 = 4p(y - k)$ and $(y - k)^2 = 4p(x - h)$.

$(y - 1)^2 = -\frac{7}{8}(x - 6)$ matches the standard form

$(y - k)^2 = 4p(x - h)$. Solve for (h, k) and p.

$x - h = x - 6 \qquad y - k = y - 1$

$\qquad h = 6 \qquad\qquad k = 1 \qquad$ The vertex is at $(6, 1)$.

$(y - k)^2 = 4p(x - h)$ and $(y - 1)^2 = -\frac{7}{8}(x - 6)$,

so $-\frac{7}{8} = 4p \rightarrow p = -\frac{7}{32}$

By definition, the focus $= (h + p, k) \rightarrow ([6 + (-\frac{7}{32})], 1)$

$= (5\frac{25}{32}, 1)$.

By definition, the directrix is $x = h - p \rightarrow x = 6 - (-\frac{7}{32})$

$= 6\frac{7}{32}$.

The axis of symmetry is parallel to the x-axis at $y = 1$. Sketch the graph, using the axis of symmetry, the vertex, the directrix, and the focus as guides.

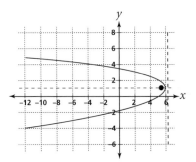

Directions Find the vertex, focus, and directrix for each parabola. Describe the axis of symmetry.

1. $(x + 3)^2 = 8(y - 2)$ _____

2. $(x - 4)^2 = 8(y + 3)$ _____

3. $(x + 4)^2 = 4(y + 3)$ _____

4. $(y + 4)^2 = 4(x - 3)$ _____

5. $(y + 1)^2 = \frac{7}{8}(x + 4)$ _____

Eccentricity

EXAMPLE

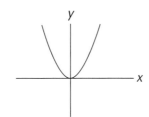

The graph is that of a parabola. Parabolas have eccentricity $e = 1$.

Directions State the eccentricity of each graph $e = 0$, $0 < e < 1$, $e = 1$,
or $e > 1$.

1. _____

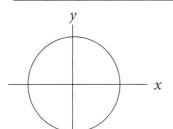

3. _____

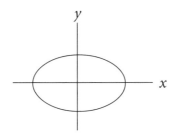

5. _____

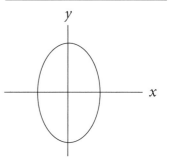

2. _____

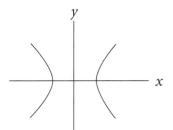

4. _____

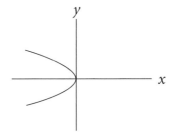

Directions Give the eccentricity of the graph of the equation. (Do not
graph.) Write $e = 0$, $0 < e < 1$, $e = 1$, or $e > 1$.

6. $(y - 9)^2 = 16x$ _____

7. $\frac{(x - 4)^2}{36} + \frac{(y + 6)^2}{81} = 1$ _____

8. $(x - 4)^2 + (y + 6)^2 = 81$ _____

9. $\frac{(x - 4)^2}{36} - \frac{(y + 6)^2}{1} = 1$ _____

10. $(y - 2)^2 = -32(x + 6)$ _____

Geometry Connection: Intersections

EXAMPLE

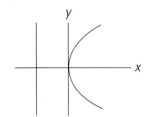

No common solutions. The parabola and straight line will not meet.

Directions Tell if the graphs have common solutions.
Give reasons for your answer.

1. _____

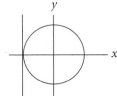

5. _____

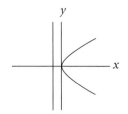

9. _____

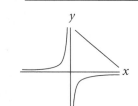

13. _____

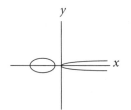

2. _____

6. _____

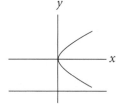

10. _____

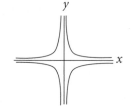

14. _____

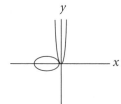

3. _____

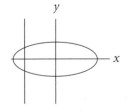

7. _____

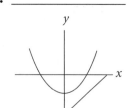

11. _____

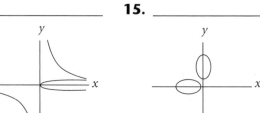

15. _____

4. _____

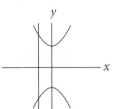

8. _____

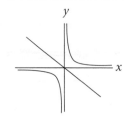

12. _____

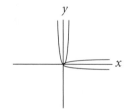

Trigonometric Ratios of the Right Triangle

EXAMPLE   Which trigonometric ratio for angle A is represented by $\frac{adjacent}{opposite}$?

Solution: $\frac{adjacent}{opposite}$ is defined as cotangent A.

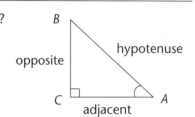

Directions   Identify the trigonometric ratio for angle A.

1. $\frac{opposite}{hypotenuse}$ _____

2. $\frac{adjacent}{hypotenuse}$ _____

3. $\frac{adjacent}{opposite}$ _____

4. $\frac{hypotenuse}{adjacent}$ _____

5. $\frac{hypotenuse}{opposite}$ _____

EXAMPLE   Give the ratio for sin D.

Solution: $\sin D = \frac{d}{f}$

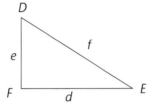

Directions   Write the ratio for each.

6. $\cos D$ _____

7. $\sin E$ _____

8. $\tan E$ _____

9. $\cot E$ _____

10. $\tan D$ _____

11. $\cos E$ _____

12. $\cot D$ _____

EXAMPLE   Name the ratio $\frac{f}{d}$ for angle D.

Solution: $\frac{f}{d} = \frac{hypotenuse}{opposite}$ for angle D = cosecant D = csc D

Directions   Referring to the triangle in the second example, identify the ratio for the given angle.

13. $\frac{f}{e}$ for angle D _____

14. $\frac{d}{e}$ for angle E _____

15. $\frac{d}{e}$ for angle D _____

16. $\frac{d}{f}$ for angle D _____

17. $\frac{e}{f}$ for angle E _____

18. $\frac{e}{d}$ for angle E _____

19. $\frac{e}{f}$ for angle D _____

20. $\frac{f}{d}$ for angle E _____

Degrees and Radians

EXAMPLE Name the quadrant that contains the terminal side of an angle that measures 210°.

Solution: Q III

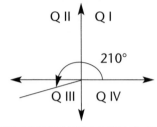

Directions Write the quadrant that contains the terminal side of each angle.

1. 5° _____

2. 310° _____

3. 150° _____

4. 70° _____

5. 215° _____

6. 125° _____

7. 110° _____

8. 205° _____

9. 40° _____

10. 255° _____

11. 350° _____

12. 290° _____

13. 55° _____

EXAMPLE Determine the range of angles that have their terminal side in Quadrant I.
Solution: 0° < angle < 90°

Directions Describe the range of angles in the given quadrant.

14. Quadrant II _____

15. Quadrant IV _____

EXAMPLE Change $\frac{2\pi}{3}$ radians to degrees.

Solution: 2π radians = 360°

$\frac{360°}{3} = 120°$

Directions Change radians to degrees.

16. $\frac{\pi}{9}$ _____

17. $\frac{\pi}{6}$ _____

18. $\frac{\pi}{4}$ _____

19. $\frac{\pi}{3}$ _____

20. $\frac{3\pi}{8}$ _____

21. $\frac{5\pi}{6}$ _____

22. $\frac{5\pi}{8}$ _____

23. 5π _____

24. $\frac{5\pi}{3}$ _____

25. $\frac{4\pi}{3}$ _____

Special Angles

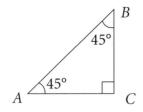 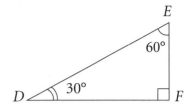

EXAMPLE   If $\overline{AB}$ is 40 ft, how long is $\overline{AC}$?

Solution: $\dfrac{\overline{AC}}{\overline{AB}} = \dfrac{\text{adj}}{\text{hyp}} = \cos A = \dfrac{\sqrt{2}}{2}$

$\dfrac{\sqrt{2}}{2} = \dfrac{\overline{AC}}{40}$; $40\sqrt{2} = 2\,\overline{AC}$; $\overline{AC} = 20\sqrt{2} \approx 28.28$ ft

Directions   Find the measures indicated. Use your calculator and round
            to the nearest hundredth.

1. $\overline{AB} = 80$ m, $\overline{BC} =$ _____

2. $\overline{BC} = 150$ ft, $\overline{AB} =$ _____

3. $\overline{BC} = 120$ ft, $\overline{AC} =$ _____

4. $\overline{BC} = 120$ mi, $\overline{AB} =$ _____

5. $\overline{AC} = 120$ mm, $\overline{AB} =$ _____

6. $\overline{DE} = 90$ mm, $\overline{EF} =$ _____

7. $\overline{DE} = 100$ ft, $\overline{DF} =$ _____

8. $\overline{DE} = 140$ m, $\overline{EF} =$ _____

9. $\overline{DE} = 60$ in., $\overline{DF} =$ _____

10. $\overline{FE} = 14$ in., $\overline{DF} =$ _____

11. $\overline{FD} = 10$ ft, $\overline{EF} =$ _____

12. $\overline{FD} = 10$ ft, $\overline{ED} =$ _____

13. $\overline{ED} = 10$ ft, $\overline{DF} =$ _____

14. $\overline{EF} = 16$ yd, $\overline{DF} =$ _____

15. $\overline{ED} = 140$ ft, $\overline{EF} =$ _____

Basic Identities

EXAMPLES   Prove the quotient identity $\tan X = \frac{\sin X}{\cos X}$, $\cos X \neq 0$.

Proof: $\tan X = \frac{x}{y}$; $\sin X = \frac{x}{z}$; $\cos X = \frac{y}{z}$

$$\frac{\sin X}{\cos X} = \frac{\frac{x}{z}}{\frac{y}{z}} = \frac{x}{y} = \tan X$$

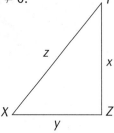

Prove the Pythagorean identity
$\sin^2 X + \cos^2 X = 1$
Proof: $z^2 = x^2 + y^2$

$$\frac{z^2}{z^2} = \frac{x^2}{z^2} + \frac{y^2}{z^2}$$

$$1 = (\tfrac{x}{z})^2 + (\tfrac{y}{z})^2$$

$$1 = \sin^2 X + \cos^2 X$$

Directions Prove each identity. Use ΔXYZ from the example.

1. Quotient identity: $\cot X = \frac{\cos X}{\sin X}$, $\sin X \neq 0$ _____

2. Reciprocal identity: $\frac{1}{\cos Y} = \sec Y$, $\cos Y \neq 0$ _____

3. Reciprocal identity: $\frac{1}{\sec 60°} = \cos 60°$ _____

4. Reciprocal identity: $\frac{1}{\tan Y} = \cot Y$, $\tan Y \neq 0$ _____

5. Reciprocal identity: $\frac{1}{\cot 30°} = \tan 30°$ _____

6. Quotient identity: $\tan Y = \frac{\sin Y}{\cos Y}$, $\cos Y \neq 0$ _____

7. Pythagorean identity: $1 + \cot^2 Y = \csc^2 Y$ _____

8. Pythagorean identity: $\tan^2 X + 1 = \sec^2 X$ _____

9. Pythagorean identity: $\sin^2 45° + \cos^2 45° = 1$ _____

10. Pythagorean identity: $\tan^2 60° + 1 = \sec^2 60°$ _____

The Unit Circle—Trigonometric Functions

EXAMPLE   Determine the reference angle of 220°.
Solution: Use the angle formed by the x-axis and the
terminal side of the angle. 220° − 180° = 40°

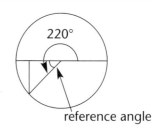

reference angle

Directions Sketch the angle in the unit circle. Then determine the
reference angle.

1. 55°   _____

3. 280°   _____

5. 165°   _____

2. 195°   _____

4. 320°   _____

EXAMPLE   What is the positive angle equivalent to −160°?
Solution: 360° − 160° = 200°

Directions Give the equal, positively-measured angle for each.

6. −55°   _____

8. −80°   _____

10. −165°   _____

7. −195°   _____

9. −320°   _____

EXAMPLE   At which x-value is the $|y\text{-value}|$ greatest?
Solution: The greatest y-value is 1.
The $|y\text{-value}|$ is 1 at $-\frac{\pi}{2}, \frac{\pi}{2},$ and $\frac{3\pi}{2}$.

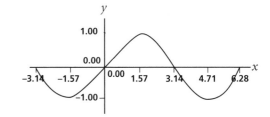

Directions Answer the questions about the graph.

11. At what x-values does the sine curve pass from negative
to positive values?   _____

12. In which quadrants is the sine curve positive?   _____

13. In which quadrants is the sine curve negative?   _____

14. At which x-values is sin x = 0?   _____

15. Using the graph, predict another x-value for which sin x = 0.   _____

Inverse Trigonometric Functions

EXAMPLE   Solve for y. $y = \sin^{-1} \frac{1}{2}$

Solution: You are looking for an angle y whose sine ratio is $\frac{1}{2}$.

You know that $\sin 30° = \frac{1}{2}$. You also know that the principal value will be

between 0 and π. Therefore $y = \sin^{-1} \frac{1}{2} = 30°$, $0 \le y \le \pi$.

Directions   Solve for y. Give principal values only.

1. $y = \sin^{-1} \frac{\sqrt{2}}{2}$ _____

2. $y = \tan^{-1} 1$ _____

3. $y = \tan^{-1} \frac{\sqrt{3}}{3}$ _____

4. $y = \sin^{-1} 1$ _____

5. $y = \cos^{-1} \frac{\sqrt{2}}{2}$ _____

6. $y = \tan^{-1} (-1)$ _____

EXAMPLE   Use your calculator to find $y = \arcsin (0.7071)$ in degrees and radians.

Solution: To find the value in degrees: Press MODE.

Choose Degree and press ENTER CLEAR . Press 2nd SIN⁻¹ 0.7071 ENTER .

Display will read 44.999... Round to 45; arcsin (0.7071) ≈ 45°.

To find the value in radians: Press MODE. Choose Radian and press ENTER CLEAR .

Press 2nd SIN⁻¹ 0.7071 ENTER . Display will read .7853... Round to 0.79 radian.

Directions   Find the value of y in both degrees and radians.

Use a calculator.

7. $y = \arcsin (0.8660)$ _____   **12.** $y = \arctan (-0.5773)$ _____

8. $y = \arcsin (1)$ _____   **13.** $y = \arcsin (-0.8660)$ _____

9. $y = \arctan (-1.732)$ _____   **14.** $y = \arctan (-3)$ _____

10. $y = \arccos (-0.7071)$ _____   **15.** $y = \arctan (3)$ _____

11. $y = \arccos (0.5)$ _____

Cofunctions and Complementary Angles

EXAMPLE Show that the equality sin B = cos A is true.

Solution: sin $B = \frac{b}{c}$, cos $A = \frac{b}{c}$; $\frac{b}{c} = \frac{b}{c}$

Therefore, sin B = cos A.

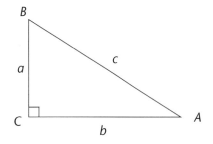

Directions Show the following equalities. Use $\triangle ABC$ from the example.

1. tan A = cot B _____

2. sin A = cos B _____

3. tan B = cot A _____

4. sec B = csc A _____

5. sec A = csc B _____

EXAMPLE Complete the equality to make it true. sin 30° = cos ___?___

Solution: sin θ = cos 90° − θ, so sin 30° = cos 90° − 30° = cos 60°

Directions Complete the equalities to make true statements.

6. sin 60° = cos _____

7. sin 45° = cos _____

8. tan 60° = cot _____

9. sec 30° = csc _____

10. sin 25° = cos _____

11. cos 40° = sin _____

12. cot 85° = tan _____

13. cot 20° = tan _____

14. sin 85° = cos _____

15. sec 50° = csc _____

Arbitrary Triangles—Law of Sines

EXAMPLE

Example: Find side *b*.

Solution: $\frac{\sin B}{b} = \frac{\sin A}{a}$; $b \sin A = a \sin B$; $b = \frac{a \sin B}{\sin A}$

$b = \frac{12 \sin 65°}{\sin 50°}$

≈ 14.20 ft

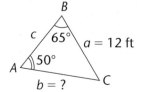

Directions Use the Law of Sines to find the missing measurement.
Round your answer to the nearest hundredth.

1.
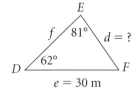

2.

H
i 70° $g = ?$
G   30°
$h = 10$ cm   I

3.

K
$l = 240$ yd   55° j
J   62°
$k = ?$ L

_____   _____   _____

EXAMPLE

Find ∠*A*.

Solution: $\frac{\sin A}{a} = \frac{\sin C}{c}$; $c \sin A = a \sin C$; $\sin A = \frac{a \sin C}{c}$

$\sin A = \frac{(15 \sin 85°)}{25} \approx 0.5977$

$\sin^{-1} 0.5977 \approx 36.71°$

$c = 25$ m   B $a = 15$ m
A   ?   85°   C
   b

Directions Use the Law of Sines to find the missing angle measure.
Round your answer to the nearest hundredth.

4.
E
$f = 55$ ft   52° d
D   ?   F
$e = 75$ ft

5.
H
$i = 12$ in.   ? $g = 44$ in.
G h I
10°

6.
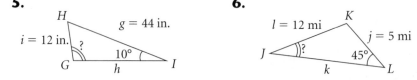

_____   _____   _____

Directions Solve the triangle.

7.
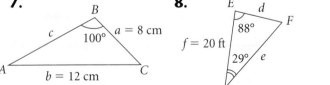

8.
E d
$f = 20$ ft   88°   F
29° e
D

9. Find ∠*Y*.
X
10 m   15°   9 m
   9 m
W   60°
Z   Y

10. Find $\overline{WZ}$.

_____   _____   _____   _____

Arbitrary Triangles—Law of Cosines

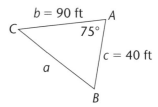

EXAMPLE   A triangle has sides of 90 ft and 40 ft; the included angle is 75°. What is the length of the third side?

Solution: Substitute values in the Law of Cosines.
$$a^2 = b^2 + c^2 - 2bc \cos A$$
$$a^2 = 90^2 + 40^2 - 2(40)(90)(\cos 75°)$$
$$a^2 = 7836.50; \; a = 88.52 \text{ ft}$$

Directions   Sketch the information. Then use the Law of Cosines to find the length of the third side. Round your answer to the nearest hundredth.

1. A triangle has sides of 30 in. and 60 in.; the included angle is 50°.   _____

2. A triangle has sides of 12 m and 15 m; the included angle is 50°.   _____

3. A triangle has sides of 12 in. and 5 in.; the included angle is 117°.   _____

4. A triangle has sides of 75 mm and 52 mm; the included angle is 93°.   _____

5. A triangle has sides of 25 yd and 15 yd; the included angle is 55°.   _____

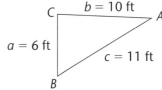

EXAMPLE   A triangle has sides of 6 ft, 10 ft, and 11 ft. What is the measure of the angle opposite the smallest side?

Solution: Substitute values in the Law of Cosines.
$$6^2 = 10^2 + 11^2 - 2(10)(11)\cos A$$
$$\cos A \approx 0.8409; \; A = \cos^{-1}(0.8409) \approx 32.76°$$

Directions   Sketch the information. Then use the Law of Cosines to find the measurement of the desired angle. Round your answer to the nearest hundredth.

6. A triangle has sides of 40 ft, 50 ft, and 70 ft. What is the measure of the angle opposite the longest side?   _____

7. A triangle has sides of 10 ft, 100 ft, and 98 ft. What is the measure of the angle opposite the longest side?   _____

8. A triangle has sides of 40 m, 90 m, and 88 m. What is the measure of the angle opposite the longest side?   _____

9. A triangle has sides of 11 ft, 12 ft, and 15 ft. What is the measure of the angle opposite the shortest side?   _____

10. A triangle has sides of 20 yd, 13 yd, and 8 yd. What is the measure of the angle opposite the longest side?   _____

Additional Identities

EXAMPLE   If $\sin \theta = \frac{3}{8}$ in Q I, what is $\sin 2\theta$?

Solution: $\cos \theta = \frac{\sqrt{55}}{8}$ and $\sin 2\theta = 2(\sin \theta)(\cos \theta) = 2(\frac{3}{8})(\frac{\sqrt{55}}{8}) = \frac{3\sqrt{55}}{32}$

Directions Use the double angle identities to complete these calculations.

1. $\sin \theta = -\frac{4}{5}$ in Q III; what is $\cos 2\theta$? _____

2. $\cos \theta = \frac{5}{13}$ in Q IV; what is $\sin 2\theta$? _____

3. $\cos \theta = \frac{5}{13}$ in Q IV; what is $\tan 2\theta$? _____

4. $\sin \theta = \frac{3}{5}$ in Q II; what is $\sin 2\theta$? _____

5. $\sin \theta = \frac{3}{5}$, $\cos \theta = \frac{4}{5}$; what is $\sin 2\theta$? _____

EXAMPLE   Evaluate $\cos 15°$.

Solution: $\cos 15° = \cos (45° - 30°)$

$= (\cos 45°)(\cos 30°) + (\sin 45°)(\sin 30°)$

$= (\frac{\sqrt{2}}{2})(\frac{\sqrt{3}}{2}) + (\frac{\sqrt{2}}{2})(\frac{1}{2})$

$= \frac{\sqrt{6}}{4} + \frac{\sqrt{2}}{4}$

$= \frac{(\sqrt{6} + \sqrt{2})}{4}$

Directions Use the appropriate identities and the values of the
trigonometric functions of 30°, 45°, and 60° to evaluate
the following.

6. $\cos 105°$ _____

7. $\tan 15°$ _____

8. $\sin 75°$ _____

9. $\sin 105°$ _____

10. $\sin 15°$ _____

Geometry Connection: Chords and Arcs

EXAMPLE Rectangle *ABCD* is inscribed in a circle; angle 1 = 35°.
Find the following measures.

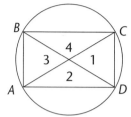

∠3 = ?   ∠3 = 35° because vertical angles are equal.

∠2 = ?   ∠2 = 180° − 35° = 145° because adjacent angles
are supplementary.

$\overset{\frown}{CD}$ = ? $\overset{\frown}{CD}$ = 35° because an arc and its central angle are equal.

Directions Find the measures of the angle and arcs.

1. ∠4 _____

2. $\overset{\frown}{BC}$ _____

3. $\overset{\frown}{AB}$ _____

4. $\overset{\frown}{AC}$ _____

Directions Use the figure at the right to answer items 5–10.
∠1 = ∠2 = ∠3

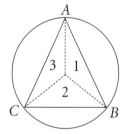

5. m∠1 = ? _____

6. m∠2 = ? _____

7. $\overset{\frown}{AC}$ = ? _____

8. $\overset{\frown}{AB}$ = ? _____

9. $\overset{\frown}{ABC}$ = ? _____

10. m∠1 + m∠3 = ? _____

Directions Complete the following sentences.

11. A figure inscribed in a circle has 45° in each arc. How many sides does _____
the figure have? Sketch the figure.

12. A figure inscribed in a circle has 18° in each central angle. _____
How many sides does the figure have?

13. An inscribed figure has four equal arcs. Sketch the figure. _____

14. What is the measure of each central angle of the arcs in the figure _____
described in item 13? Why?

15. What is the sum of two adjacent angles in the figure for item 13? _____
Explain.

The Fundamental Counting Principle

EXAMPLE   Mariah likes to snowboard and downhill ski. At the local ski resort there are
2 chairlifts to the top of the mountain. From the top, there are 4 ski runs that go
all the way to the bottom. In how many different ways can Mariah get up and
down the mountain?

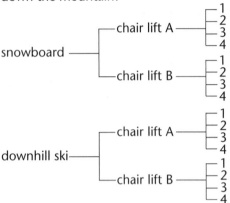

Fundamental Counting Principle: $2 \times 2 \times 4 = 16$ different ways

---

Directions Make a tree diagram and calculate the total number of possible options.

1. Suppose you toss 3 coins. If each coin can land on heads or tails,
how many different outcomes are possible?   _____

2. Greg is planning a large dinner banquet. Guests have a choice of
chicken, fish, or steak for their main course; potatoes or rice for a side
dish; and mixed vegetables, green salad, or coleslaw as a vegetable.
How many dinner combinations can be made?   _____

Directions Use the fundamental counting principle to solve each problem.

3. Hunter has 3 soccer trophies, 4 basketball trophies, 9 tennis trophies,
and 6 golf trophies. How many different ways can he arrange the
trophies in a row on his shelf?   _____

4. A yogurt shop sells yogurt in 3 different sizes. They have 16 flavors
of yogurt, 15 kinds of toppings, and 8 different flavored syrups to
choose from. How many different kinds of yogurt sundaes can you
make with one topping and one kind of syrup?   _____

5. Raul is flying from San Francisco to Missoula, Montana. Three
different airlines fly to Missoula. Each airline offers 8 flights a day.
Raul can choose between first class, business class, or coach class.
How many different travel arrangements can Raul make?   _____

Permutations

EXAMPLE   Evaluate 7! using your calculator.

Press 7 [MATH] [◀] 4 [ENTER] . The display reads *5,040.*

Directions Evaluate.

1. 1!   _____   **5.** 5!   _____

2. 2!   _____   **6.** 6!   _____

3. 3!   _____   **7.** 8!   _____

4. 4!   _____   **8.** 10!   _____

EXAMPLE   Write 7! in the form $n(n - 1)!$

7(6!)

Directions Write in the form $n(n - 1)!$

9. 1!   _____   **13.** 5!   _____

10. 2!   _____   **14.** 6!   _____

11. 3!   _____   **15.** 8!   _____

12. 4!   _____   **16.** 10!   _____

EXAMPLE   How many 7-digit numbers can be made using the numbers 0–6 without repeating digits? With repeating digits?

Without repeating digits: $_7P_7 = 7! = 5,040$

With repeating digits: $(7)(7)(7)(7)(7)(7)(7) = 823,543$

Directions Solve to find the total number of permutations.

17. How many ways can 8 different glass beads be strung on a bracelet? _____

18. In a sailboat race, 4 boats are headed for the finish line. In how many different ways can the 4 boats finish the race? _____

19. Three six-sided number cubes are tossed. How many different number combinations are possible? _____

20. If 6 six-sided number cubes are tossed, how many different number combinations with no numbers repeated can be formed? _____

Permutations: *n* Objects *r* at a Time

EXAMPLE   Evaluate $_{11}P_{11}$, using the factorial function on your calculator.
Press 11 [MATH] [◄] 4 [ENTER]. The display reads *39,916,800*.

Directions Evaluate, using the factorial function on your calculator.

1. $_2P_2$ _____   **5.** $_9P_9$ _____

2. $_3P_3$ _____   **6.** $_{10}P_{10}$ _____

3. $_4P_4$ _____   **7.** $_{12}P_{12}$ _____

4. $_6P_6$ _____   **8.** $_{20}P_{20}$ _____

EXAMPLE   Evaluate $_8P_3$ using your graphing calculator.
Press 8 [MATH] [◄] 2 3 [ENTER]. The display reads *336*.

Directions Evaluate $_nP_r$, using your graphing calculator.

9. $_5P_4$ _____   **13.** $_8P_2$ _____

10. $_7P_2$ _____   **14.** $_4P_2$ _____

11. $_9P_5$ _____   **15.** $_{20}P_{10}$ _____

12. $_{10}P_7$ _____   **16.** $_{20}P_2$ _____

EXAMPLE   A baseball coach must choose 3 of his 9 players to play in the all-star game.
How many different sets of 3 players can he make?

$$_9P_3 = \frac{9!}{(9-3)!} = \frac{(9)(8)(7)(6!)}{(6!)} = (9)(8)(7) = 504$$

The coach can make 504 different 3-player teams.

Directions Solve each problem. You may use your calculator.

17. There are 8 players on the Central basketball team and 5 different positions
to play. How many ways can the coach fill the 5 different positions?   _____

18. A baseball coach is deciding how to arrange the batting order of his 9 starting
players. How many different batting orders are possible?   _____

19. How many different ways can the letters in the word *factor* be arranged?   _____

20. Long ago, ships sent coded messages to other ships by displaying a sequence of
different-shaped flags. If a ship had a collection of 10 differently shaped flags,
how many different messages of a four-flag sequence could be made?   _____

Combinations

EXAMPLE

Of 7 students whose speeches won an award, 3 of the students will be asked to present their speeches in public. How many ways can the 3 presenters be chosen?

$_7C_3 = \binom{7}{5} = \frac{7!}{(7-3)!3!} = \frac{(7)(6)(5)(4)(3)(2)(1)}{(4)(3)(2)(1)(3)(2)(1)} = 35$

Directions Evaluate. Do not use your calculator.

1. $\binom{8}{5}$ _____

2. $\binom{7}{2}$ _____

3. $\binom{10}{8}$ _____

4. $\binom{4}{2}$ _____

5. $\binom{6}{4}$ _____

6. $\binom{6}{2}$ _____

7. $\binom{9}{3}$ _____

8. $\binom{9}{6}$ _____

9. $\binom{10}{4}$ _____

EXAMPLE

For a set having 8 elements, calculate the number of subsets having 6 elements. Use your calculator.

Press 8 MATH ◄ 3 6 ENTER. The display reads *28*.

Directions For a set having 10 elements, calculate the number of subsets having the number of elements indicated.

10. 4 _____

11. 1 _____

12. 7 _____

13. 5 _____

14. 9 _____

15. 6 _____

16. 3 _____

17. 8 _____

18. 2 _____

EXAMPLE

A set of 12 elements can be arranged in how many combinations of 5 elements?

$\binom{12}{5} = \frac{12!}{(7!)(5!)} = \frac{(12)(11)(10)(9)(8)(7!)}{(7!)(5!)}$

$= \frac{(12)(11)(10)(9)(8)}{(5)(4)(3)(2)(1)} = (11)(9)(8) = 792$

Directions Solve each problem. You may use your calculator.

19. A coach must choose 7 starting players from her roster of 11 team members. How many different combinations of starting players can she make? _____

20. How many different 5-card hands can be made from a deck of 52 playing cards? _____

Samples with Replacements

EXAMPLE   A combination lock has a five-digit code. You can use any of the
digits 0 through 9 with repetition for the code. How many possible
codes are there?

$10^5 = 100,000$

Directions Answer the questions. All problems are with replacement.

1. How many 3-digit area codes can be made with the digits
   0 through 9?   _____

2. If area codes were changed from 3-digit to 4-digit numbers,
   how many more area codes would be made available?   _____

3. How many 5-character PIN numbers can be made that contain
   2 letters followed by 3 digits?   _____

4. In a certain city, all phone numbers begin with one of 5
   different 3-digit exchanges. How many different telephone
   numbers are possible for this area?   _____

5. In the city in problem 4, how many new 3-digit exchanges
   would need to be added to allow for a total of 120,000
   phone numbers?   _____

Basic Probability

On the spinner shown here, each number is equally likely to occur.
What is the probability of spinning an even number?

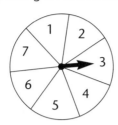

There are seven possible outcomes. Three of the outcomes, 2, 4, and 6,
are favorable outcomes. The probability of spinning an even number
is 3 out of 7, or $\frac{3}{7}$.

P(even number) $= \frac{3}{7}$

Directions Use the spinner in the example above to complete problems
1–5. Find the probability of each event.

1. spinning an odd number _____

2. spinning a number greater than 3 _____

3. spinning a number less than 3 _____

4. spinning a 3 _____

5. not spinning a 3 _____

EXAMPLE Calculate the probability of the complementary event, $P(E')$, when $P(E) = \frac{2}{3}$.

$P(E) = \frac{2}{3}$ and $1 - \frac{2}{3} = \frac{1}{3}$, so $P(E') = \frac{1}{3}$.

Directions Calculate the probability of the complementary event E'.

6. $P(E) = \frac{1}{5}$ _____

7. $P(E) = \frac{1}{6}$ _____

8. $P(E) = \frac{5}{8}$ _____

9. $P(E) = 1$ _____

10. $P(E) = \frac{x}{4}$ _____

Binomial Theorem/Combinations Formula

EXAMPLE Expand $(x^2 - 3)^4$.

$(x^2 - 3)^4 = \binom{4}{0}x^4 + \binom{4}{1}x^3(-3) + \binom{4}{2}x^2(-3)^2 + \binom{4}{3}x(-3)^3 + \binom{4}{4}(-3)^4$

$= x^4 + 4x^3(-3) + 6x^2(9) + 4x(-27) + 81$

$= x^4 - 12x^3 + 54x^2 - 108x + 81$

Directions Expand the binomials.

1. $(x + 1)^5$ _____

2. $(x - 1)^6$ _____

3. $(x + y)^8$ _____

4. $(3x - y)^5$ _____

5. $(a - b)^4$ _____

EXAMPLE Find the number of terms in the expansion of $(x - 10)^8$.

The expansion of $(x + y)^n$ has $n + 1$ terms. Therefore, the expansion of $(x - 10)^8$ has $8 + 1$, or 9, terms.

Directions Find the number of terms in the expansion of the binomials.

6. $(x - 6)^7$ _____

7. $(3a + 4)^6$ _____

8. $(x - 2y)^{12}$ _____

9. $(4m + 6)^9$ _____

EXAMPLE Find the fifth term in the expansion of $(x - y)^7$.

$n = 7; r = 5$, so $r - 1 = 4$

$\binom{n}{r-1} = \binom{7}{4} = \frac{7!}{4!(7-4)!} = \frac{7!}{4!3!} = 35$

$35(x^{n+1-r}y^{r-1}) = 35x^3y^4$

The fifth term in the expansion of $(x - y)^7$ is $35x^3y^4$.

Directions Find the term indicated.

10. 4th term of $(x + 1)^5$ _____

11. 3rd term of $(3x + 2y)^4$ _____

12. 5th term of $(a + 2)^6$ _____

13. 6th term of $(a + 2b)^{10}$ _____

14. 5th term of $(2x - y)^8$ _____

15. 6th term of $(a^2 - 2b^3)^7$ _____

Arithmetic Sequences and Series

EXAMPLE Tell whether the series $\frac{1}{2} + 1 + \frac{3}{2} + 2 + \frac{5}{2} + \ldots$ is arithmetic or not.

$1 - \frac{1}{2} = \frac{1}{2}; \frac{3}{2} - 1 = \frac{1}{2}; 2 - \frac{3}{2} = \frac{1}{2}; \frac{5}{2} - 2 = \frac{1}{2}$

Yes, the series is arithmetic. The common difference, d, is $\frac{1}{2}$.

Directions Tell whether each series is arithmetic or not. Write *yes* or *no*.
If *yes*, give the value of d, the common difference.

1. $5 + 3 + 1 + -1 + -3 + -5 + -7 + -9 + \ldots$ _____

2. $2 + 4 + 8 + 16 + 32 + \ldots$ _____

3. $10 + 20 + 30 + 40 + 50 + \ldots$ _____

4. $7.5 + 7.2 + 6.9 + 6.6 + 6.3 + \ldots$ _____

5. $2.2 + 3.0 + 3.2 + 4.0 + 4.2 + 5.0 + 5.2 + \ldots$ _____

EXAMPLE Find S_{10} for the series $3 + 6 + 9 + 12 + 15 + \ldots$

$S_n = \frac{n}{2}(a_1 + a_n); n = 10; a_1 = 3; a_{10} = 30$

$S_{10} = \frac{10}{2}(3 + 30) = 5(33) = 165$

Directions Find the sum of each series.

6. $5 + 10 + 15 + 20 + 25 + \ldots + 65$ _____

7. $-33 + -25 + -17 + -9 + -1 + 7 + 15 + 23 + 31 + 39$ _____

8. $\frac{3}{4} + 1 + \frac{5}{4} + \frac{3}{2} + \frac{7}{4} + 2 + \frac{9}{4} + \frac{5}{2} + \frac{11}{4}$ _____

9. $128 + 71 + 14 + -43 + -100 + -157$ _____

10. $1 + 3 + 5 + \ldots + 39$ _____

Geometric Sequences and Series

EXAMPLE   Find the last term in the geometric sequence 2, 4, 8, 16, . . . , a_{10}.

$a_n = a_1 r^{(n-1)}$; $n = 10$; $r = 2$; $a_1 = 2$

$a_{10} = 2(2^9) = 2(512) = 1,024$

Directions Find the last term of each geometric sequence.

1. 1, 3, 9, 27, . . . , a_{10} _____   **4.** $-3, 1, -\frac{1}{3}, \frac{1}{9}, \ldots, a_9$ _____

2. 2, -2, 2, -2, 2, . . . , a_{12} _____   **5.** $12, -6, 3, -\frac{3}{2}, \ldots, a_8$ _____

3. 2, -2, 2, -2, 2, . . . , a_{13} _____

EXAMPLE   Find the sum of $3 + 6 + 12 + 24 + \ldots + a_{10}$.

$S_n = \frac{a_1(1 - r^n)}{(1 - r)}$; $a_1 = 3$; $r = 2$; $n = 10$

$S_{10} = \frac{3(1 - 2^{10})}{1 - 2} = \frac{3(1 - 1,024)}{-1} = \frac{3(-1,023)}{-1} = 3,069$

Directions Find the sum of each geometric series.

6. $3 + 6 + 12 + 24 + \ldots + a_{12}$ _____   **9.** $100 + 50 + 25 + \frac{25}{2} + \ldots + a_8$ _____

7. $2 + 4 + 8 + \ldots + a_6$ _____   **10.** $-3 + 1 + -\frac{1}{3} + \frac{1}{9} + \ldots + a_6$ _____

8. $1 + 3 + 9 + 27 + \ldots + a_{10}$ _____

EXAMPLE   Find the geometric mean of 3 and 12. Write the sequence.

$m = \sqrt{(3)(12)} = \sqrt{36} = 6$

The geometric mean between 3 and 12 is 6.

3, (3)(2), (3)(2²) = 3, 6, 12

Directions Find the geometric mean of the number given.
               Write the sequence.

11. 2 and 18   _____

12. 3 and 27   _____

13. 1 and 100   _____

14. 2 and 200   _____

15. x and y _____

Sigma Notation—Infinite Series

EXAMPLE   Write out the terms of the series $\sum\limits_{n=1}^{4} n^3$.

$$1^3 + 2^3 + 3^3 + 4^3 = 1 + 8 + 27 + 64$$

Directions   Write out the terms of each series.

1. $\sum\limits_{n=0}^{7} n^3$

4. $\sum\limits_{m=0}^{5} (-1)^m (4k)$

2. $\sum\limits_{n=1}^{7} (-2)^n$

5. $\sum\limits_{m=1}^{4} (\frac{1}{2})^{m-1}$

3. $\sum\limits_{k=0}^{4} (2k + 2)$

EXAMPLE   Find the sum of the convergent geometric series $\sum\limits_{n=0}^{\infty} \frac{1}{3}^{n}$.

$$r = \frac{1}{3};\ a_1 = 1$$

$$\lim_{n \to \infty} S_n = \frac{1}{1 - \frac{1}{3}} = \frac{1}{\frac{2}{3}} = \frac{3}{2}$$

Directions   Find the sum of each convergent geometric series.

6. $\sum\limits_{n=0}^{\infty} (\frac{1}{2})^n$

9. $\sum\limits_{k=1}^{\infty} 2(0.1)^{(k-1)}$

7. $\sum\limits_{k=1}^{\infty} (\frac{1}{3})^{(k+1)}$

10. $\sum\limits_{n=1}^{\infty} (-\frac{1}{3})^{(n+2)}$

8. $\sum\limits_{k=1}^{\infty} (\frac{1}{10})^{(k-1)}$

Geometry Connection: Limits

EXAMPLE Write the limit of the measure of ∠Y as the measure of ∠X approaches 30°.

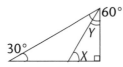

As the measure of ∠X decreases to 30°, the measure of ∠Y increases to 60°.
In symbols: $\lim\limits_{m\angle X \to 30°} m\angle Y = 60°$

Directions Use the figure in the example above to write the following limits.

1. $m\angle Y$ as $m\angle X \to 45°$ _____

2. $m\angle Y$ as $m\angle X \to 0°$ _____

Directions Use the figure below to write a limit statement for items 3–5.

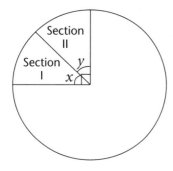

3. The area of section II as $m\angle Y$ approaches 180°   _____

4. The area of section II as $m\angle Y$ approaches 90°   _____

5. The area of section I as $m\angle X$ approaches 120°   _____

Complex Number Plane

EXAMPLE Write each number as a complex number.

5, −8, $\frac{3}{4}$, 4i

$$5 = 5 + 0i$$
$$-8 = -8 + 0i$$
$$\frac{3}{4} = \frac{3}{4} + 0i$$
$$4i = 0 + 4i$$

Directions Write each number as a complex number.

1. 9 _____

2. −2 _____

3. $\frac{2}{5}$ _____

4. $-\frac{7}{8}$ _____

5. 8.3 _____

6. −9.7 _____

7. 10i _____

8. $\frac{4}{5}i$ _____

9. 15 _____

10. 0.4i _____

EXAMPLE Give the complex number represented by point K in the graph below.
x-component = real part
y-component = imaginary part
K = 2 + −2i = 2 − 2i

Directions Write the complex number for each point.

11. A _____

12. B _____

13. C _____

14. D _____

15. E _____

16. F _____

17. G _____

18. H _____

19. I _____

20. J _____

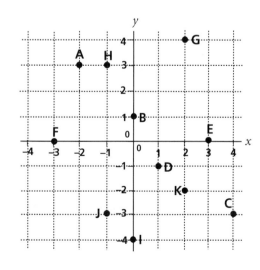

Complex Numbers: Operations

EXAMPLE   Find the sum of $(4 + 5i) + (2 + i)$.

$(4 + 5i) + (2 + i) = (4 + 2) + (5i + i) = 6 + (5 + 1)i = 6 + 6i$

Directions Find the sums of the complex numbers.
Write your answer as a complex number.

1. $(5 + 3i) + (9 + i)$ _____

2. $(6 + 2i) + (4 + 3i)$ _____

3. $(10 + 7i) + (8 - i)$ _____

4. $(3 - 5i) + (-4 + 2i)$ _____

5. $(7 - 12i) + (1 - 6i)$ _____

6. $(\frac{1}{2} + 5i) + (2\frac{1}{2} - 3i)$ _____

7. $(14 - 6i) + (6 - 10i)$ _____

8. $(-4 - i) + (-8 - 6i)$ _____

EXAMPLE   Find the difference of $(7 + 5i) - (3 - 2i)$.

$(7 + 5i) - (3 - 2i) = (7 - 3) + (5i + 2i) = 4 + (5 + 2)i = 4 + 7i$

Directions Find the differences of the complex numbers.
Write your answer as a complex number.

9. $(8 + 3i) - (6 + 5i)$ _____

10. $(7 + i) - (5 + 3i)$ _____

11. $(3 - 10i) - (-2 + 3i)$ _____

12. $(9 + 3i) - (-15 - 2i)$ _____

13. $(2 + i) - (2 + 5i)$ _____

14. $(8.5 + 0.3i) - (3.5 - i)$ _____

15. $(7 - i) - (17 - i)$ _____

16. $(6 - 4i) - (3 + 6i)$ _____

EXAMPLE   Find the product of $(3 + i)(5 - i)$.

$$(3 + i)(5 - i) = 3(5 - i) + i(5 - i)$$
$$= 15 - 3i + 5i - i^2$$
$$= 15 + 2i + 1$$
$$= 16 + 2i$$

Directions Find the products of these complex numbers.

17. $(6 + 2i)(4 + 3i)$ _____

18. $(10 - 6i)(10 - 6i)$ _____

19. $(7 + 2i)(1 - 3i)$ _____

20. $(4 - 5i)(7 + 8i)$ _____

Complex Conjugates and Division

EXAMPLE Write the conjugate of $(6 + 2i)$.
The conjugate of $(6 + 2i)$ is $(6 - 2i)$.

Directions Write the conjugate of each given complex number.

1. $(3 + 5i)$ _____

2. $(6 + 7i)$ _____

3. $(-2 + 9i)$ _____

4. $(\frac{1}{2} + \frac{3}{5}i)$ _____

5. $(8 - 4i)$ _____

6. $(3.5 - 6i)$ _____

EXAMPLE Multiply the complex number $(5 + 3i)$ by its conjugate.
$(5 + 3i)(5 - 3i) = 25 - 9i^2 = 25 + 9 = 34$

Directions Multiply the complex number by its conjugate.

7. $(1 + 3i)$ _____

8. $(8 - 6i)$ _____

9. $(5 + 2i)$ _____

10. $(\frac{1}{2} + 2i)$ _____

11. $(6 - 4i)$ _____

12. $(-7 - 5i)$ _____

EXAMPLE Find the quotient of $(4 + 2i)$ divided by $(3 + i)$.

$$\frac{(4 + 2i)}{(3 + i)} = \frac{(4 + 2i)(3 - i)}{(3 + i)(3 - i)}$$
$$= \frac{14 + 2i}{9 - i^2}$$
$$= \frac{14 + 2i}{10}$$
$$= \frac{14}{10} + \frac{2i}{10}$$
$$= \frac{7}{5} + \frac{1}{5}i$$

Directions Divide.

13. $\frac{(5 + i)}{(3 + 2i)}$ _____

14. $\frac{(6 - 3i)}{(2 - i)}$ _____

15. $\frac{(3 - 3i)}{(4 + 3i)}$ _____

Proof by Induction

EXAMPLE

Prove $1^2 + 2^2 + 3^2 + 4^2 + \ldots + n^2 = \frac{n(n+1)(2n+1)}{6}$

First, prove true for $n = 1$: $\frac{1(1+1)(2+1)}{6} = \frac{(2)(3)}{6} = 1$

Second, assume that it is true for $n = k$.

$1^2 + 2^2 + 3^2 + 4^2 + \ldots + k^2 = \frac{k(k+1)(2k+1)}{6} = \frac{2k^3 + 3k^2 + k}{6}$

Third, show that the statement is true for $k + 1$.

$1^2 + 2^2 + 3^2 + 4^2 + \ldots + k^2 + (k+1)^2 = \frac{2k^3 + 3k^2 + k}{6} + (k+1)^2$

$= \frac{2k^3 + 3k^2 + k}{6} + \frac{6(k+1)^2}{6}$

$= \frac{2k^3 + 3k^2 + k + 6(k^2 + 2k + 1)}{6}$

$= \frac{2k^3 + 9k^2 + 13k + 6}{6}$

$= \frac{(k+1)(k+2)[2(k+1)+1]}{6}$

Therefore, $1^2 + 2^2 + 3^2 + 4^2 + \ldots + n^2 = \frac{n(n+1)(2n+1)}{6}$ for all n.

Directions Prove the following by mathematical induction. Show each step.

1. $1^3 + 2^3 + 3^3 + \ldots + n^3 = \frac{n^2(n+1)^2}{4}$

Step 1 _____

Step 2 _____

Step 3 _____

2. $1 + 3 + 5 + \ldots + (2n-1) = n^2$

Step 1 _____

Step 2 _____

Step 3 _____

3. $\frac{1}{(1)(2)(3)} + \frac{1}{(2)(3)(4)} + \frac{1}{(3)(4)(5)} + \ldots + \frac{1}{n(n+1)(n+2)} = \frac{n(n+3)}{4(n+1)(n+2)}$

Step 1 _____

Step 2 _____

Step 3 _____

Addition and Subtraction of Functions

EXAMPLES Use algebra to find the sum and the difference of $f(x) = x^2 + 2$ and $g(x) = x + 1$.

$$f(x) + g(x) = (x^2 + 2) + (x + 1)$$
$$= x^2 + x + 3$$

$$f(x) - g(x) = (x^2 + 2) - (x + 1)$$
$$= x^2 - x + 1$$

Directions Given $f(x) = x^2 - 2$ and $g(x) = 4x + 1$, calculate the following.

1. $f(x) + g(x), x = 2$ _____

2. $f(x) - g(x), x = -1$ _____

3. $f(x) + g(x), x = -2$ _____

4. $f(x) + g(x), x = 0$ _____

5. $f(x) - g(x), x = 3$ _____

6. $f(x) - g(x), x = 10$ _____

7. $f(x) + g(x), x = 5$ _____

8. $f(x) - g(x), x = -8$ _____

9. $f(x) + g(x), x = 4$ _____

10. $f(x) - g(x), x = -4$ _____

11. $f(x) + g(x), x = \frac{1}{2}$ _____

12. $f(x) - g(x), x = -\frac{1}{2}$ _____

13. $f(x) - g(x), x = -10$ _____

EXAMPLE Sketch the sum of $f(x) + g(x)$.

$$f(x) = x^2; g(x) = 1$$
$$f(x) + g(x) = x^2 + 1$$

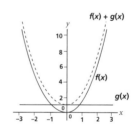

Directions Sketch the sum or difference on the coordinate plane.

14. $f(x) + g(x)$

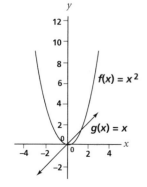

15. $f(x) - g(x)$

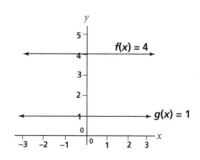

Multiplication and Division of Functions

EXAMPLE Given $f(x) = x^2$ and $g(x) = x - 3$, write the product $f(x)g(x)$ as one function.

$f(x)g(x) = x^2(x - 3) = x^3 - 3x^2$

Directions Write the product as one function, $f(x)g(x)$.

1. $f(x) = x^2 - 4, g(x) = -x$ _____

2. $f(x) = x + 3, g(x) = 2x$ _____

3. $f(x) = -2x, g(x) = x^2 + 1$ _____

4. $f(x) = x^2, g(x) = 4x + 3$ _____

5. $f(x) = x^2 + 1, g(x) = x - 2$ _____

EXAMPLE Write the quotient of $f(x) = x^2$ divided by $g(x) = x - 3$ as one function, $\frac{f(x)}{g(x)}$.

$\frac{f(x)}{g(x)} = \frac{x^2}{x - 3}$

Directions Write the quotient as one function, $\frac{f(x)}{g(x)}$.

6. $f(x) = x^2 - 2, g(x) = x + 1$ _____

7. $f(x) = 2x - 1, g(x) = 3x^2$ _____

8. $f(x) = 2x + 3, g(x) = 5x^2$ _____

9. $f(x) = x^2 + 3, g(x) = 6x + 1$ _____

10. $f(x) = x - 1, g(x) = x + 1$ _____

Calculations with Functions

EXAMPLES   What x-values must be excluded from $f(x) = \frac{1}{4x}$ and $\frac{f(x)}{g(x)} = \frac{x^2}{3x+1}$?

For $f(x) = \frac{1}{4x}$, $x \neq 0$.

For $\frac{f(x)}{g(x)} = \frac{x^2}{3x+1}$, $3x + 1 \neq 0 \rightarrow 3x \neq -1 \rightarrow x \neq -\frac{1}{3}$

Identify the <u>values</u> of x for which the function $f(x) = \sqrt{x+2}$ will be real-valued.
If $f(x) = \sqrt{x+2}$, any value of x for which $x + 2$ is less than 0 is not a real number.
Therefore, $x + 2 < 0$ or $x < -2$ must be excluded.

Directions   Tell which values of x must be excluded so that the function
has real values.

1. $f(x) = 5 - \frac{1}{2}x$ _____

2. $f(x) = \frac{x^2}{2x+1}$ _____

3. $\frac{f(x)}{g(x)}$ where $f(x) = 2x^2$ and $g(x) = x + 4$ _____

4. $\frac{g(x)}{f(x)}$ where $f(x) = 3x$ and $g(x) = 5x + 2$ _____

5. $\frac{f(x)}{g(x)}$ where $f(x) = x + 3$ and $g(x) = x^2 - 4$ _____

6. $f(x) = 3\sqrt{x}$ _____

7. $f(x) = \frac{8}{x^2+3}$ _____

8. $f(x) = \frac{3}{x^2-2}$ _____

9. $\frac{f(x)}{g(x)}$ where $f(x) = 8x$ and $g(x) = \sqrt{x-4}$ _____

10. $f(x)g(x)$ where $f(x) = 8x$ and $g(x) = \sqrt{x-4}$ _____

Composition of Functions

EXAMPLE

$f(x) = x^2 + 3$, $g(x) = x - 5$
Calculate $f(g(3))$.
$f(g(3)) = f(3 - 5) = f(-2) = (-2)^2 + 3 = 4 + 3 = 7$

Directions Given $f(x) = x - 4$ and $g(x) = x^2 + 2$, calculate the
composite functions.

1. $f(g(0))$ _____

2. $g(f(2))$ _____

3. $f(g(2))$ _____

4. $f(g(5))$ _____

5. $g(f(1))$ _____

6. $f(g(-2))$ _____

EXAMPLE

Given $f(x) = x + 4$ and $g(x) = x^2 - 2$.
Calculate $f(g(x))$ and $g(f(x))$.
$f(g(x)) = f(x^2 - 2) = x^2 - 2 + 4 = x^2 + 2$
$g(f(x)) = g(x + 4) = (x + 4)^2 - 2 = x^2 + 8x + 16 - 2 = x^2 + 8x + 14$

Directions Calculate the composite function, using the two given
functions.

7. Given $f(x) = x^2$ and $g(x) = 4x + 3$

    a. $f(g(x))$ _____

    b. $g(f(x))$ _____

8. Given $f(x) = x^2 + 1$ and $g(x) = 2x$

    a. $f(g(x))$ _____

    b. $g(f(x))$ _____

9. Given $f(x) = x + 3$ and $g(x) = x^2 - 1$

    a. $f(g(x))$ _____

    b. $g(f(x))$ _____

10. Given $f(x) = 2x + 3$ and $g(x) = x^2 - 1$

    a. $f(g(x))$ _____

    b. $g(f(x))$ _____

Geometry Connection: The Complex Plane

EXAMPLE Change 1 + i to trigonometric form.

Solution: 1 + i = 1 + 1i. Change to r(cos θ + i sin θ).

Find r. $r^2 = x^2 + y^2 = 1^2 + 1^2 = 2; r = \sqrt{2}$

Solve for θ: $\cos θ = \frac{adj}{hyp} = \frac{1}{\sqrt{2}}$

$(\frac{1}{\sqrt{2}})(\frac{\sqrt{2}}{\sqrt{2}}) = \frac{\sqrt{2}}{2}$. So $\cos θ = \frac{\sqrt{2}}{2}$ and θ = 45°.

$r(\cos θ + i \sin θ) = \sqrt{2}(\cos 45° + i \sin 45°).$

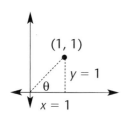

Directions Change the complex coordinates to trigonometric form.

1. $2\sqrt{3} + 6i$ _____

2. $\frac{\sqrt{3}}{2} + 3i$ _____

3. $\frac{3}{2} - \frac{3\sqrt{3}i}{2}$ _____

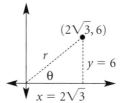
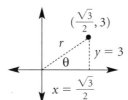
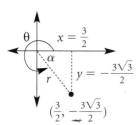

EXAMPLE Change 10(cos 330° + i sin 330°) to algebraic form.

Solution: Locate the point. Because θ = 330°, the point is in Q IV.

Reference angle = 360° − 330° = 30°

$\cos 30° = \frac{adj}{hyp} = \frac{x}{10}$, so $x = 10 \cos 30° = 10(\frac{\sqrt{3}}{2}) = 5\sqrt{3}$

$\sin 30° = \frac{opp}{hyp} = -\frac{y}{10}$ so $y = -10 \sin 30° = -10(\frac{1}{2}) = -5$

$x + yi = 5\sqrt{3} - 5i$

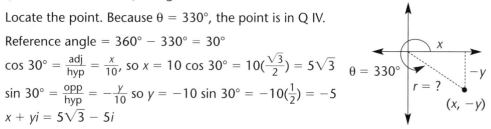

Directions Change these complex numbers to algebraic form.

4. 6(cos 120° + i sin 120°) _____

5. 4(cos 30° + i sin 30°) _____

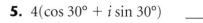
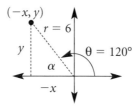

Precision and Units of Measure

$\boxed{\text{EXAMPLE}}$ Identify the number and unit in the measurement.
The snake is 5 feet long.
The snake is measured in feet, so the unit is feet.
The snake is 5 feet long, so the number is 5.

Directions Identify the number and unit in each measurement below.

1. The motor home weighs about 23,000 pounds.   _____

2. She ran in a 10 kilometer race.   _____

3. We got 1.2 inches of rain.   _____

4. My dog is $7\frac{1}{2}$ years old.   _____

5. The bottle contained 10.4 mL of medicine.   _____

$\boxed{\text{EXAMPLE}}$ A ski jumper's longest jump was 15.6 meters. What is the greatest possible error in this measurement? What is the shortest possible actual length of the jump? the longest possible actual length?

The smallest unit of measurement is 0.1 meter.
The greatest possible error is one-half of 0.1 meter, or 0.05 meter.

The shortest possible actual length of the jump is 15.6 m − 0.05 m = 15.55 m.

The longest possible actual length of the jump is 15.6 m + 0.05 m = 15.65 m.

Directions Complete the table below.

Least Possible Measurement	Measurement	Greatest Possible Measurement
6. _____	91.5 cm	**7.** _____
8. _____	$24\frac{1}{2}$ mi	**9.** _____
10. _____	6.7 kg	**11.** _____
12. _____	10.2 L	**13.** _____
14. _____	3.25 mm	**15.** _____

The Metric System

EXAMPLE | How many millimeters are in 8 cm?
1 cm = 10 mm
8 cm = (8)(10 mm) = 80 mm

Directions Write the number that makes each statement true.

1. 5 m = _____ cm

2. 3 km = _____ m

3. 6.1 mm = _____ cm

4. 79 cm = _____ m

5. 143 mm = _____ cm

6. 84.2 cm = _____ mm

7. 432 mm = _____ m

8. 10.4 m = _____ km

9. 57 m = _____ mm

10. 8,741 cm = _____ m

11. 64.6 m = _____ cm

12. 3,704 m = _____ km

Directions Solve each problem.

13. Tori grew 4.5 cm in one year. How many millimeters did she grow? _____

14. Which is shorter: 5,245 m or 52.45 km? Explain your reasoning.

_____

15. In a long jump contest, Bailey jumped 1.8 m, Morgan jumped
198 cm, and Jan jumped 1,750 mm. Arrange these jumpers in order
from longest to shortest jump.

_____

Metric Units of Capacity and Mass

Unit	milliliter	centiliter	deciliter	liter	dekaliter	hectoliter	kiloliter
Symbol	mL	cL	dL	L	daL	hL	kL
Value	0.001 L	0.01 L	0.1 L	1 L	10 L	100 L	1,000 L

Unit	milligram	centigram	decigram	gram	dekagram	hectogram	kilogram
Symbol	mg	cg	dg	g	dag	hg	kg
Value	0.001 g	0.01 g	0.1 g	1 g	10 g	100 g	1,000 g

EXAMPLES

Use the charts above to find how many liters are in 8,934 mL.

1,000 mL = 1 L

Divide by 1,000.   8,934 ÷ 1,000 = 8.934 L

Change 3.75 tons to kilograms.

1 t = 1,000 kg

Multiply by 1,000.   3.75 × 1,000 = 3,750 kg

Directions Use the charts above to answer each item.

1. How many liters are in 3,065 mL?

2. Change 8.6 L to milliliters.

3. 0.75 L equals how many milliliters?

4. Change $\frac{1}{4}$ t to kilograms.

5. Change 25.7 g to milligrams.

6. How many milliliters are in 92.3 L?

7. Change 743 mL to liters.

8. 9,043 mg equals how many grams?

9. How many tons are in 10,534 kg?

10. Change 2,184 g to kilograms.

11. 65 g equals how many milligrams?

12. 746.3 mL equals how many liters?

13. $9\frac{3}{4}$ L equals how many milliliters?

14. How many kilograms are in $\frac{2}{5}$ t?

15. Change 10,365 kg to tons.

Volume—Capacity—Mass Relation

Volume of Water		Capacity of Water		Mass of Water
1 cubic centimeter	←→	1 milliliter	←→	1 gram
1 cubic meter	←→	1 kiloliter	←→	1 metric ton

EXAMPLE

A plastic tub measures 40 cm by 20 cm by 10 cm. If the tub alone weighs 50 grams, what is the weight of the tub in kilograms when it is full of water?

Volume = 40 cm × 20 cm × 10 cm = 8,000 cm³
1 cm³ of water = 1g
8,000 cm³ = (8,000)1g = 8,000 g
8,000 g + 50 g = 8,050 g
1,000 g = 1 kg
8,050 g ÷ 1,000 = 8.05 kg
The tub weighs 8.05 kg when it is full of water.

Directions Solve each problem.

1. If lead weighs 11.4 g/cm³, how much does a lead cube with 1 cm sides weigh?

_____

2. A box has dimensions of 80 cm by 40 cm by 30 cm. What is the capacity of the box in kiloliters?

_____

3. Mercury weighs 13.69 g/cm³. If a thermometer holds 2.1 mL of mercury, what is the weight of the mercury?

_____

4. A 10 L gas can weighs 850 g when it is empty. If gasoline weighs 0.69 g/cm³, what is the weight of the gas can when it is full of gas?

_____

5. How much more does a 27 cm³ container full of water weigh than the same 27 cm³ container full of oil?
(Remember, oil weighs 0.918 g/cm³.)

_____

U.S. Customary Units of Measure

Length	Capacity	Weight (Mass)
1 foot = 12 inches 1 ft = 12 in.	1 cup = 8 fluid ounces 1 c = 8 fl oz	1 pound = 16 ounces 1 lb = 16 oz
1 yard = 3 feet 1 yd = 3 ft	1 pint = 2 cups 1 pt = 2 c	1 ton = 2,000 pounds 1 T = 2,000 lb
1 yard = 36 inches 1 yd = 36 in.	1 quart = 2 pints 1 qt = 2 pt	
1 mile = 1,760 yards 1 mi = 1,760 yd	1 gallon = 4 quarts 1 gal = 4 qt	
1 mile = 5,280 feet 1 mi = 5,280 ft		

EXAMPLE The wingspan of a certain bald eagle is 92 inches. What is its wingspan in feet?
12 inches = 1 foot
93 inches ÷ 12 = 7 R9, or 7 feet 9 inches
$\frac{9}{12}$ = 0.75
So, the eagle's wing span is 7.75 ft.

Directions Solve each problem.

1. The soccer field at the community park is 55 yards long. How many feet long is the field? _____

2. How many 6-ounce servings of punch are in a 1-gallon punch bowl? _____

3. Mt. Everest is 29,028 feet above sea level. About how many miles is that? Round your answer to the nearest half-mile. _____

4. How many yards of duct tape are needed to tape around a box whose length is 8 feet and width is $5\frac{1}{2}$ feet? _____

5. A double-decker streetcar is 140 inches high. Can the streetcar fit under a railroad bridge that is 11 feet 4 inches high? Explain your reasoning.

Time and Rate Conversions

EXAMPLE A worker earns $570 each week. The worker works 6 hours a day,
5 days a week. What is the worker's hourly wage?

Total hours worked = (5)(6 hours) = 30 hours

$570 ÷ 30 h = hourly wage

$$\frac{\$570}{30\ h} = \frac{\$19}{1\ h}$$

The hourly wage is $19.00 per hour.

Directions Solve each problem.

1. Alicia spends 40 minutes a day driving to work and back. If she
works 250 days a year, how many hours per year does she spend
driving to work and back? Round your answer to the nearest hour. _____

2. Referring to problem 1, calculate how many days Alicia spends
driving to work and back per year? Round your answer to the
nearest day. _____

3. An ostrich can run at a speed of 39 miles per hour. How many miles
per minute is this? How many miles per second? _____

4. A worker earns a monthly salary of $2,400. If the worker works
8 hours a day, 20 days a month, what is the worker's hourly wage?
What is the daily wage? _____

5. A certain study reveals that, on average, teenage boys play 1.25 hours
of video games per day. How many days in a year do they play video
games? Round your answer to the nearest day. _____

Organizing and Displaying Data

EXAMPLES   Display the data below in a frequency table, stem-and-leaf plot, and histogram.

Data

Ages of participants			
45	28	35	19
12	43	41	33
20	30	15	18
52	25	51	16
30	45	56	68

Frequency Table

Ages of participants		
Interval	Tally	Frequency
10–19	⦀⦀	5
20–29	⦀⦀⦀	3
30–39	⦀⦀⦀⦀	4
40–49	⦀⦀⦀⦀	4
50–59	⦀⦀⦀	3
60 and above	⦀	1

Stem-and-Leaf Plot

Ages of participants	
1	2 5 6 8 9
2	0 5 8
3	0 0 3 5
4	1 3 5 5
5	1 2 6
6	8

Histogram

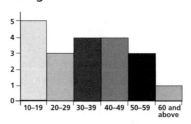

Directions   Consider the data in the chart at the right. Display the data as directed.

1. Display the data in a stem-and-leaf plot.

2. Display the data in a frequency table.

3. Display the data in a histogram.

Number of books read during contest			
18	7	22	17
20	6	24	18
10	23	5	21
19	14	17	11
3	11	16	23

Directions   Use the data displays you made in items 1, 2, and 3 above to answer these questions.

4. Which of the three displays do you feel is the best way to show the given data? Explain your reasoning.

_____

5. How are a frequency table and a stem-and-leaf plot similar? How are they different?

_____

Central Tendency: Mean, Median, Mode

EXAMPLE   Find the range, mean, median, and mode of the set of data.

{3, 7, 8, 4, 3, 9, 4, 5, 7, 10, 7, 5}

Order the data from least to greatest.

3	3	4	4	5	5	7	7	7	8	9	10

range: $10 - 3 = 7$

mean: $3 + 3 + 4 + 4 + 5 + 5 + 7 + 7 + 7 + 8 + 9 + 10 = 72; 72 \div 12 = 6$

median: $\frac{(7 + 5)}{2} = 6$

mode: 7

Directions   Use the data set below to complete items 1–4.

{10, 12, 8, 22, 7, 13, 9, 6, 5, 8, 13, 8}

1. What is the range of the data set?   _____

2. What is the mean of the data set?   _____

3. What is the median of the data set?   _____

4. What is the mode of the data set?   _____

Directions   Create your own set of data containing at least 10 pieces of data. Use your data set to answer questions 5–8.

5. What is the range of the data set?   _____

6. What is the mean of the data set?   _____

7. What is the median of the data set?   _____

8. What is the mode of the data set?   _____

Directions   Consider the data set below. Then answer the questions.

{18, 17, 18, 18, 14, 20, 16, 16, 19, 17, 18, __?__ }

9. Assume that a value of 36 is added. How will the mean change?   _____

10. How will the mode change? Explain.

Geometry Connection: Three Dimensions

EXAMPLE   What is the location of point *F*?
Point *F* is at $x = 30$, $y = 0$, $z = 50$. $F = (30, 0, 50)$

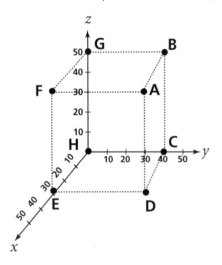

Directions Use the diagram above to answer the questions.

1. What is the location of point *D*?   _____

2. What point is located at $(0, 40, 0)$?   _____

3. What is the location of point *A*?   _____

4. What point is located at $(0, 40, 50)$?   _____

5. What is the location of point *H*?   _____